YANKEES, TYPEWRITERS, SCANDALS, AND COOPERSTOWN

A Baseball Memoir

Bill Madden

Library of Congress Cataloging-in-Publication Data

Names: Madden, Bill, author.
Title: Yankees, typewriters, scandals, and Cooperstown: a baseball memoir
 / Bill Madden.
Description: Chicago, Illinois: Triumph Books LLC, [2025]
Identifiers: LCCN 2024037625 | ISBN 9781637277157 (cloth)
Subjects: LCSH: Madden, Bill, author. | Baseball writers—United
 States—Biography. | New York Yankees (Baseball team)—History.
Classification: LCC GV742.42.M33 A3 2025 | DDC 796.357092
 [B]—dc23/eng/20241105
LC record available at https://lccn.loc.gov/2024037625

This book is available in quantity at special discounts for your group or organization. For further information, contact:
 Triumph Books LLC
 814 North Franklin Street
 Chicago, Illinois 60610
 (312) 337-0747
 www.triumphbooks.com

Printed in U.S.A.
ISBN: 978-1-63727-715-7
Design by Nord Compo
Photos courtesy of Bill Madden unless otherwise indicated

For Charlie Madden, who weaned me on baseball and sportswriting but never got to see the fruits of his encouragement, and Muriel Madden, who always supported.

CONTENTS

FOREWORD

In 1985 I was managing the Oneonta Yankees in the New York–Penn League—my first managing job—when the team owner, Sam Nader, told me he was taking me to the Hall of Fame in nearby Cooperstown, New York, for the annual induction ceremony. I later found out this was a tradition of Sam's—to take his manager to the Hall of Fame inductions. "There's someone I especially want you to meet," Sam told me.

That "someone" was Bill Madden, who by then had been the New York Yankees beat writer for the *New York Daily News* for nearly eight years. "Bill is a special friend," Sam told me. "He's the best baseball writer in New York, and you need to get to know him. He knows the Yankees organization inside and out."

When Sam introduced us, he said: "Bill, I want you to meet my manager. I want you to take good care of him when he gets to New York."

Sam obviously had a lot more confidence in me than I did, but when I finally did work my way up through the Yankees system—first as their third-base coach in 1990 and then as manager in 1992—a relationship with Bill Madden had started that has withstood the demand of both our jobs for almost 40 years and been one of mutual respect and admiration.

When "The Stick," Gene Michael, hired me to manage the Yankees in 1992, we talked about all the writers covering the team, and in particular Bill with whom he was good friends away from the field. "Billy's one guy you can trust," Stick said. "He's a dogged reporter and he's been around the team a long time and knows everybody in the organization."

It was about the same thing Sam Nader had told me seven years earlier. Bill's knowledge and respect of the game and pure love of the competition always got my attention. A question coming from Bill in a pregame or postgame press conference I knew was gonna be based on his tireless homework and pursuit of being accurate, fair—and most times—first.

After I left the Yankees in 1995, I always welcomed Bill's presence in the clubhouses of all the teams I managed subsequently. Here was a guy with whom I could confide in about my teams and whose opinions I valued. It seemed wherever I went, I encountered baseball people who had a tremendous respect for him. The first was Roland Hemond, the vice president of the expansion Arizona Diamondbacks, and that team was my second Major League Baseball managing job. Roland was such a positive influence for me in Arizona, having experienced some horrible losing teams and then quick turnarounds as general manager of the Chicago White Sox in the early '70s and the Baltimore Orioles in the late '80s. He was maybe the most beloved baseball executive the game has ever known, but as he told me after Bill had come to visit the Diamondbacks camp in spring training in 1998: "Bill Madden is more than just a longtime friend. He's the best baseball writer in the country with a deep knowledge of the history of the game."

I had already come to see Bill's knowledge of the game and its history in all his writings for the *Daily News* when I was with the Yankees. He has always had a passion for bringing his readers inside the game within the game, and this especially comes out in his latest endeavor.

I've always enjoyed his take on anything in the baseball world, knowing it would be tough but fair. *He gets it.* I'm talking about the human element that is the fabric of our game, the pureness of spring training, the grind of a regular season, and the passion and sense of urgency of a postseason playoff. All of that is here in this informative and highly entertaining book—an inside look at the life of a baseball writer, for which I was honored to be asked to write the foreword. Enjoy!

—*Buck Showalter*

PROLOGUE

On the morning of October 8, 1956, I was getting dressed for school when my father, Charlie Madden, peeked his head in my bedroom and announced: "Gonna be a short day at school for you today, son. I'll be picking you up at 10:00, and we're going to the World Series."

"Really?" I said. "The World Series?"

"Your first World Series," my father replied matter of factly. "We arranged it with your teacher to let you out early."

I'm not sure who—my father or me—was more thrilled with this development. Charlie Madden, who owned a plumbing supply company in Hackensack, New Jersey, had three passions in life—golf, baseball, and newspapers and he weaned me on the latter two. We had the *New York Herald-Tribune* delivered every morning to our home in Oradell, New Jersey. My father proclaimed on many occasions that the *Tribune* had the finest sports section of any paper in America under the tutelage of the legendary sports editor Stanley Woodward. The hard-bitten Woodward had both a keen eye for writing talent and nose for news and at the *Tribune* he'd assembled a staff of talented sportswriters unrivaled in New York or anywhere else. Among them were horse racing savant Joe Palmer and track and field/Olympics authority Jesse Abramson, both legends in their fields, but his prize hire was his lead columnist, Red Smith. "You need to read Red Smith every day," my father instructed. "There's no finer sportswriter in America."

And so I did. Then, as I reached my teenage years, I expanded my newspaper consumption by going downtown after lunch and buying the PM New York dailies—especially the *New York Journal-American* for the acclaimed Jimmy Cannon and the *New York World-Telegram* for the brilliant cartoons by the renowned Willard Mullin. But it took me a while to realize that a good part of my father's knowledge of baseball, which was passed on to me, was obtained indirectly from Dick Young of the *New York Daily News*.

My father scorned the *Daily News*, which he deemed a scandal rag tabloid that would never be allowed in our house. But he had no way of avoiding it at his plumbing supply company in Hackensack, where the plumbers all regularly left their copies on the counter in the mornings after deliberating over all the baseball news of the Yankees, Dodgers, and Giants and in particular Young's take on everything in his column. One of my father's regular plumbing customers was a guy named Charlie Hulley, who just happened to be Young's next-door neighbor in Woodcliff Lake, New Jersey. "You gotta read Young today, Charlie," was a daily refrain from Hulley. "Great stuff again you don't find anywhere else. He's the best."

And as time went on, my father grudgingly agreed. Young was not the eloquent wordsmith that Smith was, but he delivered a cleverly written, hard-hitting, daily dosage of meat-and-potatoes baseball news, minced with opinion, for the two million *Daily News* readers. George Vecsey, the award-winning columnist for *The New York Times*, probably best described Young's writing style as "having all the subtlety of a knee in the groin."

When I was in junior high school, my father bought me an Olympia typewriter, which I used to write my own baseball stories based on what I'd read in all the New York papers as well as the weekly *Sporting News*, and every spring I would write a team-by-team preview of the coming baseball season. One year my father asked Hulley if he could arrange a visit for us to meet Young and have him look at my latest baseball preview. Much to my father's surprise, Young agreed to meet us at his house. After some small talk about my aspirations of being a sportswriter, Young asked to look at the baseball preview piece I'd written. I can still remember standing there trembling as Young perused the piece for a few minutes before looking up and saying: "Not bad. Keep at it, kid."

All the way home in the car, my father was ecstatic. "How great was that, Billy! *Dick Young* liked what you wrote!"

I never told Young that story when, some 28 years later, he hired me at the *Daily News*. I'm sure he wouldn't have remembered it. But even after he left the *Daily News* for the *New York Post* in 1981 and until the day he died at age 69 in 1987, he never stopped being a mentor to me.

"Talk to your readers like you're having a conversation with them and always try to tell 'em something they don't know," he counseled me. "Everyone knows the score of the game. Tell 'em the stuff they didn't know from watching the game on TV. Remember, TV is our competition. And above all: don't try to be a fucking Hemmingway. You're not. You're a reporter first, and our readers are depending on that. Don't ever forget it."

By the time I got hired by the *Daily News* in 1978 after nine years of "apprenticeship" at United Press International in New York, the newspaper business was already beginning to recede. Of the seven major New York City dailies when I was growing up—the AM *Daily Mirror* and *Herald Tribune* and the PM *Journal-American* and *World-Telegram*—had all folded while the *Post*, the last of the afternoon papers, had converted to an AM edition. Thus began the decades-long New York tabloid war between the *News* and the *Post*, and all the lessons I had learned from Young were put into practice in all of my columns and game stories.

On the occasion of my being honored at the Hall of Fame as the recipient of the Baseball Writers J.G. Taylor Spink (now Career Excellence) Award in 2010, I sought to emphasize in my acceptance speech the importance of the written word and especially newspapers in the growth of baseball's popularity over the last 100 years. It was also through the many books on baseball, which I voraciously consumed as a kid—Charles Einstein's marvelous *Fireside Book of Baseball* trilogy, the 1940s to 1950s Putnam's team history series, Harold Seymour's *Baseball—The Early Years* and *Baseball: The Golden Years*, Lee Allen's *100 Years of Baseball*, to name just a few—that I was able to gain a real knowledge of the game's history.

I since tried to incorporate baseball history in all the books I've written, even Don Zimmer's autobiography, *Zim: A Baseball Life.* When we began the project, I explained to Zim, who'd been a Brooklyn Dodger and an original 1962 Met as a player, that because he had managed the Chicago Cubs and Boston Red Sox—the storied heartbreak franchises—and was finally Joe Torre's bench coach with the modern dynastic New York Yankees, he needed to be a narrator of all the game's history over the previous 50 years. "You're kind of like that 121-year-old Indian scout played by Dustin Hoffman in the movie *Little Big Man*, who was the sole survivor of the Battle of Little Big Horn," I said before quickly realizing Zimmer, who never went to the movies, had no idea what I was talking about.

Nevertheless, he had a fantastic memory of all the events of his career and whatever he didn't remember was backed up in the 50 to 60 scrapbooks his wife, Soot, had painstakingly kept up from the time they were both in high school. It made for one of the easiest, fun, and most rewarding books I've ever written.

In 2003 the New York Yankees were celebrating their 100th anniversary, but with the expected plethora of the *Yankees at 100* and *100 Years of Yankees History* books to be published that year, I wanted to write a Yankees century book that would differentiate itself from all the others. I came up with the idea of crisscrossing the country and interviewing 17 former Yankees from all different eras, going all the way back to the 1920s, plus Arlene Howard, the widow of Elston Howard, the first Black Yankee, and especially including 90-year-old Frank Crosetti in San Francisco (who set the record straight on Babe Ruth's called shot homer in the 1932 World Series). Through them I was able to write the Yankees' history firsthand from the players who made it. *Pride of October* was one my most satisfying experiences if only because of all of my "subjects"— Yogi Berra, Whitey Ford, Jerry Coleman, Lou Piniella, Bobby Murcer, Mel Stottlemyre, Don Mattingly, Joe Pepitone, Bobby Richardson among them—were so accommodating and into it and really opened up to me. (Imagine spending a day with Whitey Ford, driving around his old neighborhood in Astoria,

Queens, as he pointed out all the old fields where he'd played youth ball and the still barely visible target painted on the wall of an abandoned building where he spent countless hours practicing how to pitch.)

Jackie Robinson was nearing the end of his career when I was in grade school, and I didn't fully understand the impact he had had on baseball until the 1960s Civil Rights movement when he was front and center as one of the most forceful voices for Black equality in America. What I did later come to realize was that integration in baseball after Robinson broke the color line in 1947 had been grudgingly slow, especially in the American League where the Yankees had reigned supreme for decades.

It was not until 1954—the one year the Yankees were not in the World Series—that for the first time both teams in the World Series, the New York Giants and Cleveland Indians, had players of color: Willie Mays, Monte Irvin, and Hank Thompson on the Giants and Larry Doby on the Indians. At the same time, however, eight teams: the Philadelphia Athletics, Washington Senators, Detroit Tigers, Boston Red Sox, and Yankees in the American League and St. Louis Cardinals, Philadelphia Phillies, and Cincinnati Reds in the National League—half of baseball—still had not integrated!

There was a story there, largely ignored, that no one had written. So 50 years later, I wrote a book—*1954: The Year Willie*

Mays and the First Generation Black Superstars Changed Baseball Forever—because, upon reflection, I had concluded 1954 and not 1947 was the real breakthrough season of integration in baseball. For not only did the 23-year-old Mays electrify America with his sensational play as the National League Most Valuable Player and with his defensive heroics in the World Series, but Hank Aaron and Ernie Banks made their respective major league debuts with the Milwaukee Braves and Chicago Cubs, and Doby led the American League in homers and RBIs for an Indians team that set an American League record with 111 wins.

Fortunately for me, Irvin and the Indians' Al Rosen, though both in their early 80s, still had sharp memories of all that went on during "the year the Yankees lost the pennant" and served as my principal Giants and Indians authorities on their teams' respective drives to the pennant and the Giants' epic sweep of the Indians in the 1954 World Series. I was especially interested in exploring the improbable dynamic of the Giants, in which the nucleus of the team was composed of the three Blacks—Mays, Irvin, and Thompson—and five sons of the South, Whitey Lockman, Alvin Dark, Dusty Rhodes, Don Mueller, and Davey Williams. How was it they were so close, not just then but for the rest of their lives? And why was race never even brought up among them? (Hint: Mays.)

I was later told there were some people in the hierarchy of the Yankees, who'd previously been very supportive of me with both *Pride of October* and my biography of George Steinbrenner called *Steinbrenner: The Last Lion of Baseball*, that were displeased with *1954* because of the way it characterized the Yankees' resistant stance on integration in baseball. Certainly, the period between 1947 until 1955, when the Yankees finally brought their first Black player, Howard, to the big leagues and the rest of the American League holdout teams followed suit, did not distinguish them from a non-discrimination standpoint, but it *was* a part of their history.

Because I've written so much about the Yankees in my books and nearly 50 years for the *Daily News*, there was always the perception that I must also be a Yankees rooter. But I think I can speak for all my colleagues in the press box when I say our primary rooting interest is in good games (and as a result good stories) and I have had the benefit to have witnessed hundreds of them, starting with that day, October 8, 1956, when my first World Series game turned out to be the greatest World Series game of all time. The Yankees' Don Larsen pitched a perfect game against the Dodgers.

It was later revealed that Joe Trimble, the Yankees beat writer for the *Daily News*, froze at his typewriter in trying to come up with a lead for his story. Turning to Young, sitting next to him, Trimble said: "Can you help me, Dick?"

"Sure," Young said. "The imperfect man pitched the perfect game" in reference to Larsen having been a renowned late-night roustabout and an otherwise ordinary pitcher.

As we exited Yankee Stadium, my father could hardly contain himself. "What a game!" he exclaimed over and over. "We're all going to be famous! You'll never see another one like it, Billy."

Well, actually I did. Forty-two years later, on May 17, 1998, I found myself sitting in the Yankee Stadium press box as David Wells, who happened to have gone to the same Point Loma High School in San Diego as Larsen and who was also a notorious free spirit, pitched the second perfect game in Yankees history. I'd be lying if I said I didn't feel my father's presence next to me as I watched Wells, seemingly effortlessly, retire the Minnesota Twins in order in the sixth, seventh, eighth innings, and into the ninth with a nary a hard-hit ball and I remembered the story of Young bailing out Trimble on Larsen's gem. There was never any doubt in my mind that Wells was going to complete his masterpiece, and when he did, I sat there in silence, surrounded by this feeling of déjà vu—Wells, Larsen, my father and I, Young again—that had filled the afternoon at Yankee Stadium. It all seemed so surreal.

From 1975 until 2015, I covered nearly 40 World Series, so many memorable games involving so many baseball heroes from Johnny Bench, Joe Morgan, Carlton Fisk, Willie Stargell, and Kirby Puckett to Derek Jeter, Mariano Rivera, and Bernie Williams. But though I liked and admired all of them, they weren't *my* heroes. My heroes were the sportswriters who covered them. I considered it a privilege to sit in the same press box as the all-time giants of my profession—Smith, Shirley Povich from Washington, Bob Broeg from St. Louis, Jim Murray from Los Angeles, John Steadman from Baltimore, Furman Bisher from Atlanta. And I can think of no one who would have been more envious of my being in that company every fall than Charlie Madden.

CHAPTER ONE

COOPERSTOWN CONFIDENTIAL

Dark, foreboding clouds were closing in on Cooperstown the afternoon of July 25, 2010, when I found myself standing at the podium of the Clark Sports Center in front of a backdrop of a record 51 returning Hall of Famers, preparing to give my acceptance speech for becoming the 61st recipient of the Baseball Writers Association's J.G. Taylor Spink (now Career Excellence) Award.

I had previously covered every Hall of Fame induction since Willie Mays' in 1979, but this was the first time I was on this side of the podium, looking out at the audience and not part of them. The Career Excellence Award is the Baseball Writers Association's highest honor, and there is nothing more special than an award that is voted on by your peers—in this case the same 400 or so senior baseball writers who elect the Hall of Fame players every year.

To say the least, it was an overwhelming induction weekend for me (and thankfully the rain held off until I was finished with my speech)—and made even more so when I saw my plaque on the wall of the Hall of Fame library alongside those of all the previous winners, a veritable who's who of the greatest sportswriters in history from Damon Runyon, Ring Lardner, and Grantland Rice to Red Smith, Shirley Povich, Heywood Broun, and Jim Murray. Whenever I'd pass through the Hall of Fame library and see that gathering of plaques on the wall, I'd think of the oft-repeated line by my great friend, Don Zimmer, with whom I collaborated on two books: "What's a lifetime .235 hitter like me doing in a group like this?"

I have always considered the Hall of Fame induction to be baseball's high holy day of obligation, and thanks in no small part to Tom Seaver, the Hall of Famers themselves agree it's a day you're supposed to be there. For years a lot of the Hall of Famers chose not to return to the inductions for various reasons, but after Seaver got elected in 1992 with the highest plurality at the time (98.84 percent), he took on the role as the unofficial president of the place, personally calling all the Hall of Famers over the winter, emphasizing to them the importance of induction weekend and for showing their support for the new electees.

At the private Hall of Famers-only Sunday dinner, Seaver organized his own pitchers-only table with Bob Gibson, Sandy Koufax, Steve Carlton, Don Sutton, Ferguson Jenkins, Rollie Fingers, Phil Niekro, and Juan Marichal in which they were all required to bring an expensive bottle of wine, though none of them likely matched the $125 a bottle of Seaver's own award-winning GTS cabernet. After a couple of years, however, Seaver (reluctantly, he maintained) was forced to amend the pitchers' exclusivity at the table to include his two batterymates, Johnny Bench and Carlton Fisk. The third basemen—George Brett, Mike Schmidt, Brooks Robinson, Wade Boggs, and Paul Molitor—had their own table too in which they always included the widow of Eddie Mathews, who came back every year and was treated like one of the boys.

Seaver especially appreciated the job the Baseball Writers Association did in the Hall of Fame voting and served as the liaison between the writers and the Hall of Fame's board of directors, of which he was a member. When I received the Career Excellence Award in 2010, the writers elected only one player, Andre Dawson. When I walked into the Otesaga Hotel, where the Hall of Famers all stay, Seaver was sitting on a couch in the middle of the lobby. "Keep sending us class acts," he said to me. "Another good election by you guys."

It was a tradition the Baseball Writers Association continued to maintain right up until 2022 when they elected "Big Papi" David Ortiz (not with my vote) despite all his steroids taint and Dominican drug lord association baggage. I could only imagine how Seaver would have reviled that election.

My close relationship with Seaver did not really take root until 1984, a year after he'd returned to the New York Mets following five-and-a-half years of "exile" in Cincinnati. During his 1968–76 heyday with the Mets, I was covering the New York Yankees for the *Daily News* and didn't spend a lot of time around the Mets—and was thankfully removed from the ugly feud between Seaver, Mets president M. Donald Grant, and my *Daily News* mentor Dick Young that led to his trade to the Reds on June 15, 1977.

I was at my *Daily News* office on the morning of January 17, 1984, when I got a call from my longtime friend Art Berke, who worked in public relations at ABC sports and had previously been in the baseball commissioner's office from 1975 to 1980. "I was just wondering if you were writing anything about the draft on Friday?" he said.

The draft Berke was referring to was something called the free-agent compensation draft, which baseball created as one of the key elements of the settlement of the 1981 players strike, where teams losing premium (called Type A) free agents could be compensated by selecting a player out of a pool of hundreds of players from the 29 other clubs. It seemed Berke, who grew up in Chicago and was a lifelong White Sox fan, had a special interest in this draft because the White Sox—by virtue of losing their top reliever Dennis Lamp as a free agent to the Toronto Blue Jays that winter—had the first pick. Since neither the Yankees nor Mets had lost any free agents and therefore wouldn't be participating in the draft, I hadn't thought much about it until then. "I doubt it,

Art," I said. "Our teams didn't lose any free agents. It's not a New York story."

"Don't be so sure," he said. "It might actually be a *huge* New York story."

"What do you mean?"

Suddenly, Berke began talking very excitedly. He said he'd been talking to a friend of his in the commissioner's office who had privy to all the clubs' protected lists. His friend, knowing Berke was a White Sox fan with a particular interest in the draft, had dropped a bombshell on him. "You'll never guess who the Mets left unprotected," Berke said.

"Okay, I give up, who?

"Tom Seaver!"

As I tried processing this, Berke continued. "And not only that, the White Sox are going to take him!"

"How do you know that?" I asked him.

"Because I called one of my friends in the White Sox baseball operations, and he confirmed it to me. He said they couldn't believe their eyes when they saw Seaver's name among the unprotected players!"

After hanging up with Berke, I began pondering just how I was going to handle this news, which would become about the biggest story I would ever break in my 50 years with the *Daily News*. First, I needed to get confirmation of it by the Mets, which was going to be dicey. I called Jay Horwitz, the Mets public relations man and told him I needed to talk to Frank Cashen, the Mets general manager. Horwitz said Cashen was at a luncheon at Shea Stadium and wouldn't be back at his office for a couple of hours. "I need to talk to him *now*," I said. "It's important, very important."

"I can't call Frank out of a luncheon unless I know what this all about," Horwitz said.

"All right, I'll tell you, Jay," I said, "but if this gets out, I will personally drive over to Shea Stadium and kill you!"

"Okay, okay," Horwitz stammered. "I'll get him!"

Five minutes later Cashen called me back.

"What is it, Billy?" he said. "Jay said you have an important story you want to talk to me about?"

"Well, Frank, "I said, "I understand you guys have left Seaver off your protected list for the draft on Friday."

After a momentary silence, Cashen said: "I've known you too long, Billy. So I'm not gonna lie to you. We did leave him off the list. He's a 39-year-old pitcher out of a pool of hundreds of players, a lot of them good prospects. We didn't think anybody would take him. Plus, everybody knows he's our guy."

"That may be true, Frank," I said, "but I have it on good authority the White Sox are going to take him with the first pick."

Again, there was silence on the other end. Finally, Cashen said: "I don't know what to say. I have no comment. I guess you have to write your story and if you're right I'll just have to deal with it."

Now I had my confirmation. But before I started writing up the story, I felt I had an obligation to give Seaver a heads-up as to what was coming. It was a risky call as I didn't know him that well and I didn't know how he would react. I called his home in Greenwich, Connecticut, and he picked up the phone himself. "Tom, this is Bill Madden from the *News*."

"Oh hi, Bill," he said. "What's up?"

"Tom, I'm afraid I may be the bearer of some bad news here," I said.

"Uh, oh," he said, "what kind of bad news?"

"Well, it seems the Mets have left you off their protected list for the free-agent compensation draft Friday."

"They what?" Seaver said. "I don't understand."

I explained to him that the Mets must have figured because he was their guy, their franchise player, nobody would take him. But I continued: "I've been told that the White Sox *are* going to take you. You're going to have to leave the Mets again."

"We'll see about that," Seaver said. "I appreciate you telling me this, Bill. I've got a lot of thinking to do."

What transpired for the next 12 hours could never happen today in the age of cell phones and social media. We sat on the story all day long and held it out of all the editions of the *Daily News* until the four-star sports final, which went off the presses at 1:30 AM. The whole time I held my breath, certain it was going to leak out somehow. I figured Seaver would be calling people, and Cashen would be calling people, but amazingly neither apparently did. The next day my story was splashed across the back page of the *Daily News* under the headline "Tom Foolery" in which I wrote: "Tom Seaver, who only a year ago had thought he'd come home to stay, may be leaving again. In a daring gamble that may well blow up in their faces, the Mets have left the 39-year-old pitcher unprotected for the free-agent compensation draft."

The next day at Shea Stadium, the Mets were forced to hastily call the most embarrassing press conference in their history. Seaver and Cashen sat side by side explaining to a horde of New York media why the greatest pitcher in their history was again being forced to leave for another team. To his eternal credit, Cashen took the fall for the organization, saying: "If we felt there was even the slightest chance Tom would have been taken, I would never have brought this embarrassment on the owners of this ballclub."

Though I didn't realize it at the time, my handling of this story dramatically changed my relationship with Seaver from player/journalist to player/friend. He later told me how appreciative he was that I called him first before going to print with the story, and from that point on, we talked periodically by phone. Then in June of 1986 after two-and-a-half years in Chicago, Seaver called me from the road in Boston. "I need you to do me a favor," he said.

He explained to me how the White Sox were going nowhere that year and he felt he was just wasting away in Chicago. "I need your help. I want to come home and finish out my career in New York."

The Mets, however, were not an option as they were well on their way to the best season in their history with a full contingent of quality young starting pitchers in Dwight Gooden, Bobby Ojeda, Ron Darling, Sid Fernandez, and Rick Aguilera. "I need you to call Steinbrenner for me," Seaver continued. "My general manager here, Hawk Harrelson, is willing to trade me, but we need an intermediary with George. I need you to tell him how much I'd really like to finish my career as a Yankee."

My initial thought was this was going to be a no-brainer for Steinbrenner. Bringing back an all-time favorite player to New York and upstaging the Mets' drive to the pennant in the process? This was right out of The Boss' playbook! That's why—to this day—I never understood Steinbrenner's resistance to the deal. "George," I pleaded, "we're talking Tom

Seaver here! When he goes to the Hall of Fame, he'll have the Yankees on his plaque right next to the Mets! Think about that!" But Steinbrenner insisted Harrelson was asking too much, and Seaver ended up being traded to the Boston Red Sox. It was the one time in The Boss' life he had pangs of conscience when he had a chance to one-up the hated Mets.

I feel very fortunate to have had a lot of personal relationships (as opposed to player/writer relationships) with Seaver's Hall of Fame contemporaries. Brett and I became good friends when he realized Milton Richman, whom he adored, had been my first boss at UPI. He even gave his first son the middle name Richman after Milton and his brother Arthur. One late night in the Otesaga lounge, Brett and I both had a few cocktails when somebody (probably me) suggested we re-create Brett's infamous Pine Tar tirade at Yankee Stadium on July 24, 1983. With me assuming the role of home-plate umpire Tim McClelland (who had nullified Brett's ninth-inning, two-run, go-ahead home run off Goose Gossage because of excessive pine tar on his bat), Brett lunged at me, his eyes bulging, throwing a flurry of imaginary punches. Although it made for great last-call theater, I had to inform Brett he was still out.

Brett was inducted in the Hall of Fame in 1999 along with Nolan Ryan and Robin Yount in what was at the time the largest attendance—an estimated 50,000—in the history of the inductions. There were also the second-largest number of 34 returning Hall of Famers. The Saturday before the induction ceremony, the normal peaceful afternoon tranquility of the Otesaga was interrupted by the booming voices of Ted Williams and Tommy Lasorda who'd been engaged in a spirited debate at lunch that now continued out onto the hotel veranda where they began drawing a crowd of curious onlookers, which included former Kansas City Royals and Blue Jays catcher Buck Martinez (who was a guest of Brett's), Red Sox general manager Dan Duquette, former Spink Award-winning writer Allen Lewis (who'd served on a couple of Veterans Committees with Williams), and Maureen Cronin, the granddaughter of Red Sox Hall of Famer Joe Cronin, all wondering what all the commotion was about. Williams, meanwhile, was accompanied by his trusty aide Buzz Hamon, the director of the Ted Williams Museum in Hernando, Florida, who'd brought with him (presumably on Williams' orders) a baseball encyclopedia for the purposes of settling any and all disputes Williams got into over the weekend.

The debate had started with the two arguing over whether pitchers or hitters were dumber and later evolved into an animated (mostly from Williams' point) discussion about Shoeless Joe Jackson. Williams was a huge proponent of Shoeless Joe for the Hall of Fame and lobbied hard with different baseball commissioners to have the disgraced White Sox slugger's lifetime ban lifted for participating in the 1919 World Series fix. "If you ask me, Shoeless Joe had one of the greatest single seasons of all time in 1912," Williams said at one point.

"Ah, c'mon, Ted," Lasorda needled. "Greatest of all time? Better than Babe? Hell, better than *you*?"

"Get the book, Buzz," Williams shouted to Hamon, who scurried across the veranda to a coffee table where the encyclopedia had been placed and brought it over to Williams, who opened to the page with Shoeless Joe's record.

"Here!" Williams said, beaming. "Look at this: hit .395 and led the league with 226 hits and 26 triples. Twenty-six fucking triples! The guy did everything."

At that point, somebody in the crowd mumbled, "You know you had 14 triples yourself, Ted, in 1940."

"Oh, bullshit!" Williams boomed. "Get the book, Buzz!"

Again, Hamon retrieved the encyclopedia and this time opened it to Williams' page where, sure enough, in 1940, his second season with the Red Sox, he hit a career-high 14 triples while also scoring a league-leading 134 runs in 144 games and hitting .344 (that would ironically wind up being his lifetime average). "I'll be damned," Williams said, glancing at his record. "I never came close to that again!"

The hilarious Williams/Lasorda back-and-forth shouting match went on for almost an hour, and those in the small crowd, who bore witness to it, will never forget it. It was one of those spontaneous and cherished memories at Cooperstown when once a year all of the game's legends are gathered in one place. I only wish the Hall of Fame had someone video recording it for posterity. When they all let their hair down during the Hall of Famers' Saturday night jam sessions with the band in the Otesaga lounge, they amazed us with their singing prowess. Johnny Bench evoked his Oklahoma roots with a medley of country Western songs; Ozzie Smith did his best Sam Cooke; Kirby Puckett, handkerchief in hand wiping his face, did a dead-on impersonation of Louis Armstrong's "Wonderful World;" and Paul Molitor, a devoted Bruce Springsteen fan who traveled on tour with his E Street Band, made a huge rookie impression in his 2004 induction year with a rousing rendition of the Boss' "Glory Days." Of course, the highlight of all these jam sessions was always 80-something Stan Musial smiling and laughing with his harmonica in hand, riffing lively foot-stomping renditions of "Wabash Cannonball" and "Orange Blossom Special."

I didn't know Williams like I did so many of the other Hall of Famers, but like everyone else, I felt in awe being in his presence. Prior to that 1999 induction weekend, he'd suffered a couple of strokes, and in November of 2000, he underwent open heart surgery and never returned to Cooperstown. It was during those last couple years of his life that Williams' son, John Henry, took control of his life, closing out all of his friends in baseball, including his constant companion, Hamon, whom he fired as the Ted Williams Museum director. John Henry essentially held Ted captive in his home next to the museum in Hernando while every day bringing in hundreds of bats, balls, and stacks of photos for the old man to sign.

But as it turned out, John Henry Williams' biggest score was when Ted died at age 83 in July 2002. Sometime in the previous year, he had convinced his father to change his will and upon death allow his body to be turned over to the Alcor cryogenics firm in Scottsdale, Arizona, purportedly to preserve his DNA for further use. The minute Ted took his last breath at the hospital in Hernando, hospital officials filled his body with blood thinner and stuffed it into a bag with dry ice for transportation to the airport in Ocala, Florida. There it was loaded onto a plane chartered by Alcor for a flight to Arizona, where it was taken to their lab in Scottsdale and then frozen and stored in a cylinder filled with liquid nitrogen.

It was never revealed how much John Henry was paid by Alcor for this famous athlete's body, but he was sued by his half-sister Bobby Jo Ferrell over the changing of Ted's will. When Hamon learned of this, he was both horrified and heartbroken. Six months after Ted's body was acquired by Alcor (where it was later learned he was also beheaded), I got a call from Hamon. So distressed over what had happened to his friend, he'd been determined to see Ted's final resting place for himself, and with the help of a friend of his, Bobbie Sgrillo, a former mortician living in Phoenix, they were able to talk themselves into the Alcor facility. "After what I saw and experienced, I just can't contain myself any longer," Hamon told me. "I want the whole world to know what they've done to Ted." Besides Hamon's vivid descriptions of the grubby and unsanitary conditions in the facility, we were able to obtain photos of the giant cylinders where the frozen bodies are stored from the *East Valley Tribune*, which we ran on the back page of the February 19, 2003, editions of the *Daily News* under the huge headline "Ted's Chamber."

I told Hamon I was grateful that he chose me to share his story with and that I, too, shared his grief. But he wasn't done, he said. He was more determined than ever to free Ted from the Alcor horror chamber and have him cremated according to his wishes. "In my last conversation with him, two weeks after I left the museum, Ted said to me: 'Buzz, I need a lawyer because I've made a huge mistake,' and at that point someone apparently walked in the room and grabbed the phone out of his hand," Hamon said. "That was the last time I ever talked to him, but when I got into that room with all those cylinders, I at least felt that Ted knew I was there."

I'd hoped to have periodic follow-ups with Hamon, but on February 9, 2004, he died at his home at age 58 in Greenville, South Carolina. It was reported to be a suicide. There's no way I will ever believe that. Hamon was a man who knew too much about John Henry Williams, who himself died of leukemia at 35 in 2004, and Alcor, and for me anyway, his death will remain an unsolved mystery. In 2002 Ferrell dropped her suit over the will against John Henry and his other sister, Claudia, presumably with a financial settlement, along with a confidentiality agreement. I tried numerous times to contact Sgrillo about Hamon's death but got no response. As far as I'm concerned now, he died of a broken heart.

I've always said the true beauty of baseball, which sets it apart from all the other sports, is its lore and the storytellers who embellish that lore, of whom Williams was one of the best. Another one was Joe DiMaggio, whom I got to know as a friend through Barry Halper, the onetime limited partner in the Yankees and owner of the most extensive collection of baseball memorabilia ever assembled. DiMaggio was inducted into the Hall of Fame in 1955 and had never been back because of his intolerance for all the autograph collectors proliferating the hotel in those days. But by 1982 things had changed drastically. The Otesaga was heavily guarded with security, and Halper was able to convince DiMaggio to drive up with him and me to the inductions from New Jersey.

After making one quick stop at Yankee Stadium, where DiMaggio picked up a couple of cases of baseballs from the Yankees clubhouse man, Nick Priore, we embarked on the four-hour drive to Cooperstown with Halper as the wheel-man, me riding shotgun, and DiMaggio in the back seat, regaling us with one story after another of his playing days in the '30s and '40s. A couple of days earlier, there had been a story in the papers that Steinbrenner was considering bringing in the famous far-reaching left-center field fences at Yankee Stadium to accommodate his new right-handed slugger Dave Winfield. "Don't get me started about that," said DiMaggio before he did. "I'll never know how many home runs and extra-base hits I lost to those fences [which at their farthest were 457 feet from home plate]. But I do remember two in particular. It was late in 1937, and I was waging a duel for the RBI crown with Hank Greenberg. We had a game against the Red Sox at Yankee Stadium, and I was only about five or six RBIs behind Greenberg at the time and I came up twice in the game with bases loaded and both times hit balls deep into the left-center field alley 450 feet away. Home runs in any other park. And wouldn't you know, each time my own brother, Dom, ran both of them down and robbed me with catches on the warning track. Instead of a possible eight RBI or five or six, I got nothing! That night Dom came over to my apartment for dinner, and I didn't talk to him the whole time."

As long as he was honed in on the '30s, I took the opportunity to ask him about Lou Gehrig. "What kind of guy was Gehrig?" I asked. "He was always in the shadow of Ruth."

"Lou was the best teammate I ever had," Joe said. "He took me under his wing when I first came up in '36, and then we became fast friends. There's a lot about Lou that nobody knew."

"Really? Like what?" I pushed.

"They always said Lou was a momma's boy who drank nothing but milk and didn't run around at night," Joe said. "I'll bet you boys never knew that Lou had an affair with Mae West!"

With that revelation of the Iron Horse hooking up with the notorious Hollywood sex bomb, Halper nearly drove off the road, and all I could think of was how much I would've loved to have had a tape recorder for this conversation. I'd never seen Joe so at ease, talking freely about everything, even bringing up Marilyn Monroe a couple of times, and I got the feeling he was really looking forward to his first trip to Cooperstown in nearly 30 years. At one point we were passing through one of those tiny, five-block upstate burgs when DiMaggio spotted a Dairy Queen off in the distance. "Let's get us some ice cream," he said.

Inside, the waitress behind the counter did a double take at the sight of DiMaggio attired in a conservative dark blue suit and tie. After ordering a vanilla cone, DiMaggio excused himself to use the restroom, but when he came back and began to reach for his wallet, the waitress waved him off. "Aren't you Joe DiMaggio?" she asked.

"Yes, I am," he said.

"Oh, there's no charge," she replied.

A few minutes later as we were finishing up our cones in the parking lot, DiMaggio remarked: "You know the ice cream here is pretty good, but I don't know how they make any money in this place if they give it away."

DiMaggio was serious. He really didn't understand his magnitude, especially in these rural, in-the-middle-of-nowhere settings. On the other hand, when he went to restaurants in the city where he knew he was recognized, he fully expected them to pick up his tab.

I saw DiMaggio a lot over the next 10 years at the New York Baseball Writers dinners and all the special events (Opening Day, Old-Timers' Day, World Series) at Yankee Stadium. After the baseball memorabilia industry exploded, he would ask me and Halper to accompany him to card shows in the New York area. He was always suspicious of promoters, always wanting to make certain he was getting the top dollar for his autograph. DiMaggio spent his entire life making sure no one would ever take advantage of him and many a friend (including Halper) found themselves abruptly and forever ostracized from DiMaggio's realm when he felt they were making money off him, which is why I found it so ironic that DiMaggio had almost as sad an ending as Williams, a virtual prisoner in his own house at the mercy of a brazen opportunist who wound up making a small fortune off him.

Only instead of John Henry Williams, DiMaggio's exploiter was Morris Engelberg, a litigious Hollywood, Florida, tax attorney whom DiMaggio had entrusted with all his business affairs in the mid '80s and who later became the sole trustee for his entire multi-million-dollar estate, much of it having been accrued from his late-in-life memorabilia signing deals. In the process Engelberg succeeded in shutting out all of DiMaggio's friends (and even for a while his brother Dom) after DiMaggio entered Memorial Hospital in Hollywood on October 12, 1998, for what was pronounced to be "walking pneumonia" but what was in fact later learned to be terminal lung cancer. Although it was finally reported in December that DiMaggio had undergone cancer surgery, Engelberg kept putting out periodic glowing statements of how well he was doing, how much he was looking forward to Opening Day at Yankee Stadium, which nobody believed but couldn't confirm otherwise, throughout his 99-day hospital stay. And all the while, Engelberg would keep bringing DiMaggio baseballs and other memorabilia to sign until he got too tired.

I tried calling the hospital a couple of times, hoping that if I could only get through to him, DiMaggio would talk to me. But Engelberg had DiMaggio's phone blocked. Then one day in early February 1999, a few weeks after DiMaggio had finally been released from the hospital and moved to his house nearby, I got a call from Richard Ben Cramer, the Pulitzer Prize-winning author who was working on what would become the definitive DiMaggio biography *The Hero's Life*. During the course of his research for the book, Cramer had sought out Halper and myself for background on all of DiMaggio's memorabilia dealings with Engelberg. "You've been a big help to me," Cramer said. "Now I'm gonna give you something that I can't use 'cause my book's not coming out for another year. Joe's got lung cancer and he's dying."

"How do you know this, Richard," I said. "Are you sure?"

"More than sure," Cramer said. "I got a nurse from the hospital who tends to him every day."

"Does anyone else know about this?" I asked.

"Yeah, call Jerry Romolt," Cramer replied.

Romolt was a big-time memorabilia operator from Chicago who had done numerous lucrative signing deals with DiMaggio, and when it came to DiMaggio, he knew all. If there was anyone who could work his way around Engelberg's obstruction, it was Romolt. So I called him and asked him if he'd heard anything about Joe's condition. "It's real bad,"

Romolt said. "Morris is full of shit. Joe's dying. He's got lung cancer and in real bad shape, bedridden, on a respirator, hooked up with tubes. He doesn't have long."

I then immediately called my sports editor at the *News*, Teri Thompson, and told her what I had, and together we scrambled to craft a story reporting the Yankee Clipper was on the way out, dying of lung cancer despite all the rosy proclamations from Engelberg to the contrary. Thompson then called Debbie Krenek, the *News* editor in chief, and told her of our exclusive—and that she probably needed to keep the "wood" (aka Page One) open. That was when Krenek informed us she was under orders from *Daily News* publisher Mort Zuckerman that any stories involving DiMaggio had to first be cleared by the noted New York foot doctor to the stars Rock Positano. Besides being Zuckerman's foot doctor, Positano was also a frequent companion of DiMaggio's and bragged to everyone how tight they were. About an hour later, Thompson called me. "You're not gonna believe this," she said. "Positano says it's not true. DiMaggio's not dying and doing fine. Krenek's killing the story."

I was sick. How in hell could the *Daily News* kill a story this big on the word of some celebrity foot doctor when I was their guy and had two impeccable sources for it? I was even sicker when a couple of days later, Halper, who hated Engelberg, called me and told me he had just been at the Friars Club and run into Marvin Scott, the longtime award-winning news anchor at New York's local WPIX Channel 11, which just happened to be part of the Tribune Corporation, the parent company of the *Daily News*, and was on the 11th floor of our building. "Look Bill," Halper said. "I don't know what happened to your story on Joe, but Marvin Scott told me he has it on good authority that Joe's dying and he's going on the air with it tonight. I just wanted you to know that."

That night I watched Scott report exclusively that DiMaggio had had a cancerous tumor removed from his lung and that his condition was far worse than had been reported and that he was on a respirator. All I could think was, *Well, at least the exclusive of DiMaggio's imminent demise had been broken by someone in the Tribune Corp. family and not* The New York Times *or* New York Post.

DiMaggio died March 8, 1999, in his home in Hollywood at age 84, and the next day, there were hundreds of tributes to him. In my opinion none was more fitting than what Sparky Anderson said of him: "There ain't never been no player with as much class as Joe DiMaggio."

Ah, Sparky. The master of garbled syntax, repetitive double negatives, contradictory monologues, and often outrageous hyperbole ("Barbaro Garbey is another Roberto Clemente"), all of which belied the genius of one of the greatest managers in history—the first to win World Series in both leagues—who was elected to the Hall of Fame in 2000. There was no one who preached the gospel of baseball like Sparky. It was no wonder his idol was Casey Stengel, the Hall of Fame manager who probably just as much deserved a place in the Hall of Fame of entertainment after captivating audiences of sportswriters and baseball folk for 50 years with his own steady stream of rambling monologues on the state of the game, which came to be called "Stengelese."

For the Yankees beat writers in the '80s, our favorite city was Detroit because of Sparky. Even though the visiting clubhouse didn't open until 4:00, my fellow scribe, Moss Klein of *The Star-Ledger*, and I would get to the ballpark around 3:00 and head straight to the Detroit Tigers clubhouse where Sparky would be waiting in his office, smoking his pipe, ready to fill up our notebooks. He would talk on almost until gametime, and I often thought he'd rather shoot the bull with the writers than manage the game.

One of my all-time favorite Sparky sessions occurred in June of 1983. He had just recently achieved his 2,011th victory to surpass Leo Durocher for sixth place on the all-time list, but on this day, his mind was on Dallas Green, who was managing the Mets and presently in last place. "You never get over the losing," Sparky's spiel began. "If you can't feel the punishment from losing, then it just ain't worth it. You might as well stop taking the people's money. There's not supposed to be no joy in Mudville when your butt is getting beat. That's why Dallas has been on my mind all week. His body is taking a beating, believe me."

I loved Sparky for his brute honesty. No more so than his stance during the 1994 players strike when he defied Detroit ownership by refusing to manage replacement players, costing him $150,000 in salary and ultimately leading to the end of his 18-year tenure as Tigers manager. "There ain't no place for replacement players in baseball," he said. "I ain't no hero and I don't want no bowl of chocolate ice cream and cherries just for doing the right thing. All the money on the table was mine. Nobody matched the ante."

I will always remember the time I told him in his office: "I can't come in here anymore, Sparky, because you've got so much bullshit I'm going to have to buy myself a pair of hip boots!" He got such a kick out of that, and from that day on—whenever I'd come into his office or see him on the field or at baseball functions—he would grin at me and lift up the bottom of his pant leg.

The last time I saw Sparky was at Cooperstown in 2010, the year I was honored. It was especially sad because he was afflicted with dementia and no longer recognized people. The sparkle in his eyes was gone and replaced with a hollowness, and he had to be led around the Otesaga by Dan Ewald, the longtime former Tigers public relations man who'd helped him write his book in 1998. On the morning of the Sunday ceremonies, the Hall of Famers were all gathered in a room off the lobby of the Otesaga where they waited to board the busses to take them out to the Clark Sports Center. It was just an amazing feeling being in that room and included all that baseball royalty—if only for a day. I remember Jack O'Connell, the secretary/treasurer of the Baseball Writers Association and our own liaison with the Hall of Fame's board of directors, telling me: "Enjoy your moment in that room. It's part of the deal." As I sat there in silence, glancing around the room, my eyes fell on Sparky, sitting by himself across the way, staring blankly at the surroundings.

And all of a sudden, he spotted me, and his face brightened. He broke into a smile and then, instinctively, reached down to his ankle and lifted up his pant leg! It was one of the most beautiful moments I can ever remember in all my years as a baseball writer. Sparky died four months later on November 4 at age 76. In my obituary tribute to him, I wrote that the baseball writers were blessed to have had him for 26 years. "We will never see his like again, and when he arrives at the Pearly Gates, I do hope St. Peter has a pair of hip boots hidden away up there somewhere. Heaven knows he's going to need them."

That Sunday night after the ceremonies, I was sitting at a table near the entranceway of the Otesaga lounge with my wife, Lillian, enjoying a couple of celebratory glasses of wine, still savoring every moment of the greatest weekend of my life. It was right around midnight when the bar began clearing out, and one by one, a group of Hall of Famers—Ozzie, Niekro, Winfield, Ryne Sandberg, Sutton, Molitor, Boggs, and Jenkins—each stopped briefly at my table and said: "Welcome to the club, Bill."

As Sparky would've said: it don't get no better than that.

CHAPTER TWO

IT'S NOT WHAT
YOU KNOW...

In the summer of 1970, I was working for *The State* newspaper in Columbia, South Carolina, while in the process of finishing up the final three credits for my degree in journalism at the University of South Carolina. I had originally matriculated to South Carolina on a track scholarship, having been a two-time New Jersey state champion in the 100- and 220-yard dashes, but quickly delved into my first love—sportswriting—as a columnist for the school paper, *The Gamecock*. I primarily covered the legendary Frank McGuire's nationally ranked basketball team.

At the time there were probably no more than a couple dozen students from the New York/New Jersey area at South Carolina, eight of whom were on McGuire's basketball team. McGuire had first achieved nationwide acclaim by coaching North Carolina to an undefeated, 32–0 season in 1957 with a team of recruits mostly from New York, which the media dubbed "McGuire's Underground Railway." That year the Tar Heels won the national championship game by defeating Wilt Chamberlain's favored Kansas team in triple overtime. It remains the greatest national basketball championship game ever.

Prior to that, McGuire had taken St. John's to the NCAA championship game in 1952, losing to Kansas. After coming to South Carolina in 1964, he resumed his same "Underground Railway" formula for success that he had at North Carolina, recruiting exclusively from the New York/New Jersey area, and quickly led the Gamecocks to national prominence as well for the first time in the school's history. As such, McGuire was the man in the state of South Carolina, and as yet another New York/New Jersey transplant, I became one of Frank's boys while covering the team.

During the 1969 Christmas holidays, I was in Harry M's bar next to Madison Square Garden after a New York Rangers hockey game when I was introduced to a pleasant, moon-faced man named Dana Mozley, who happened to be the *New York Daily News'* hockey beat writer. During the course of our conversation, I told Mozley I would soon be graduating from South Carolina and asked him how I might go about getting a sportswriting job in New York. "Don't bother writing to the New York papers," Mozley said, "because they're not gonna hire somebody right out of college. What you should do is write to the wire services, the Associated Press and UPI [United Press International], which both have their main offices in New York. They cover the whole country, and being as you grew up in New Jersey and are going to school in South Carolina, you might be just the kind of guy they're looking for."

I asked Mozley if there was anyone in particular I might write to, and he gave me the name of Jack Griffin, who was the sports editor at United Press International. Before I left to return to South Carolina, I wrote Griffin a letter but never heard back from him. I completed my spring semester, then enrolled in summer school to secure those last three credits, and got a job covering sports for *The State*, which I began to assume was probably going to be my first and final destination as a sportswriter.

But then one day in August, I was sitting at my desk in *The State* sports department when the sports editor, Herman Helms, peeked out of his office and shouted: "Bill, Frank McGuire's on the phone on line two. He wants to talk to you."

Everyone in the department turned their heads and looked at me. This was the equivalent of a city-side cub reporter at the *New York Daily News* during 9/11 being told Rudy Giuliani was on the phone asking to speak to him. By then, McGuire was probably the most powerful man in the whole state. "He wants to talk to *me*?" I asked.

"Yeah, I don't know what he wants, but he asked to speak to you personally," Helms replied.

With considerable trepidation I picked up line two and said, "Hi, Coach," to which McGuire abruptly cut me off and said: "Look, Billy, I don't have a whole lot of time here, but I just got off the phone with Jack Griffin up in New York, and you've got the job."

Dumbfounded, I stammered: "Whoa, Coach, I don't know how you got involved in this. I didn't use you a reference or anything. I would've told you."

"Well, you stupid bastard, you should have," McGuire said. "Don't you know, when I was at St. John's, Jack Griffin was my ballboy?"

"I don't know what to say," I said, still shell-shocked.

"There's nothing more to say," said McGuire. "You better get on the phone to Griffin before he changes his mind."

As soon as I hung up with McGuire, I called Griffin at UPI in New York and introduced myself. "Mr. Griffin, this is Bill Madden calling from Columbia, South Carolina. Frank McGuire told me I should give you a call."

On the other end of the phone, I heard a chuckle. "Son, I want you to know that right here on my desk I must have a hundred letters like yours. We just lost one of our writers to *Newsday*, and as I was sifting through them today, I came across yours from the University of South Carolina, and that caught my eye. It gave me the opportunity to call Frank, who in my mind was the only guy on Earth who would decide whether or not I should give you this job. I asked him about you, and he said I should hire you. So, you're hired."

That was it. No clips, no resume, no letters of recommendation. Griffin was hiring me as a sportswriter at United Press International's main office in New York because Frank McGuire, the basketball coach at South Carolina, said he should. "When would I start?" I asked.

"Can you get here next week?" Griffin said. "We need someone right away."

"Well, er, I'm finishing up the last few credits for my degree…but…uh…yeah, sure, I can be there," I said.

After hanging up I went into Helms' office and told him the good news, and as I expected, he gave me a firm handshake and wished me well. He was a kind man, one of my first mentors, and a legend in his own right in Columbia, having broken numerous stories on the Gamecocks through the years while being both feared and respected by all the school's coaches.

The next day, I cleaned out my apartment, packed up my 1967 Oldsmobile Cutlass convertible, hugged my roommates, and hit the road for the 13-hour drive to New York. At the time it didn't matter to me that I was leaving the last three credits for my degree behind. I was going to the big time.

There was, however, one not-so-small issue to attend to before I could sever all my ties with South Carolina. With the Vietnam War now in full fury in the spring of 1969, I would soon be losing my 2-S college deferment, as was my college roommate, Paul Renard, who was originally from Pennsylvania. We had both tried enlisting in the Army reserves and the Coast Guard, to no avail, and had resigned ourselves to being drafted at the end of the spring semester, when Paul woke me up one morning and declared: "Good news, Madden, I can get us in the National Guard!"

"How are you going to do that?" I asked.

It seemed Paul had an aunt who was the head nurse at the local hospital in a small town just north of Charleston in South Carolina's low country. "My aunt has delivered just about every baby in the town over the last 20 years and she's a pillar of the community. One of her close friends happens to be the warrant officer in the local National Guard unit there. She told him about us, and he said he'd take us in."

The next day we were in the warrant officer's office at the armory in Paul's aunt's sleepy little town, signing all the papers that would make us official members of the South Carolina National Guard, even though neither one of us was a resident or had even been born in South Carolina—a not-so-minor detail the warrant officer made sure to drive home to us. After flipping through a stack of index cards on his desk with names and addresses and commenting to us that all of them happened to be Black—and had no chance of being accepted into his unit—he added, looking at Paul: "We don't have any Yankees in this unit either, but because of your aunt, I'm gonna make an exception for you two boys."

When we left the office, I looked at Paul and said: "Do you believe that guy? That was outrageous! What the hell have we gotten ourselves into here?"

We got more of idea when we stopped at a little convenience store on the outskirts of town that had a sign in the window, which said: "We do not refuse Negro customers here, but all the proceeds from anything they buy will go directly to the Ku Klux Klan."

To channel Dorothy on Kansas in *The Wizard of Oz*, clearly we weren't in cosmopolitan Columbia anymore but rather some backwoods burb, rife with racism, where the Civil Rights Act of 1964 had gone on deaf ears. So needless to say, it was with much trepidation that we would once a month make the hour-and-a-half drive from Columbia for our weekend training. We stayed at Paul's aunt's house and walked the short distance around the corner to the armory for 7:00 AM formation with our newfound "redneck weekend warriors," many of whom appeared to have come straight from a night of heavy partying, the pint bottles of bourbon quite visible stuffed into the rear pocket of their fatigues.

Six months later, I was in the same warrant officer's office, informing him that I had gotten a job in New York and that I needed a transfer to a National Guard unit in New Jersey.

"Transfer?" he said. "After all I did for you, letting you into this unit in the first place, now you want a *transfer*? You're not getting any transfer."

"But I'm gonna be moving to New York," I said.

"That's your problem," he said. "As far as I'm concerned, you can go to New York whenever you want, but one weekend a month, you're gonna have to be here for meetings, and two weeks every summer, you're going to have to go to summer camp with this unit."

"This isn't fair," I said. "Do I have any recourse here?"

"Well," he said, "you can talk to the adjutant general in Columbia, but I doubt if he'll give you a transfer either."

Nevertheless, when I got back to Columbia, I called over to the adjutant general's office and got an appointment. To say the least, the South Carolina adjutant general was a most intimidating figure. A huge (6'3", some 230 pounds), barrel-chested man with an Army uniform fully decorated with medals and ribbons, he looked like he could have been chairman of the joint chiefs of staff. "Well, son," he said, "just what is it that brings you here?"

I explained to him my predicament about needing a transfer and how I was told he was the only man who could give me one. "I don't know, son," he said. "I don't like superseding our local guard units. How did you get a job in New York?"

"Actually," I said, "Frank McGuire got me the job."

"Frank McGuire?" he said somewhat incredulously.

I then proceeded to tell him how I'd covered and traveled with McGuire's basketball teams the past three years. "I think Coach McGuire considered me one of his boys, and he has a lot of connections up in New York, including the sports editor at United Press International, where I've been hired."

Suddenly, there was a change in his demeanor, and I detected a softening in his stance.

"Frank McGuire, huh?" he said.

"Yes," I said. "You can call him if you want to verify this."

"I don't know if that'll be necessary," he said. "Give me a day to think about this."

The next day, the adjutant general called me back with both good news and ominous news. "Okay," he said. "You've got your transfer—with one condition. You've got to go to at least one summer camp with your unit here."

With the dreaded prospect of having to fly back to South Carolina to a fate unknown in a few weeks, I reported to UPI, located on the 12th floor of the Daily News Building at 220 East 42nd Street in late June. The moment I walked through the door, I was taken aback by the noise of hundreds of clattering teletype machines spread across the sprawling office that sounded like a gigantic army of cicada bugs. "Pardon the noise," said Griffin, extending his hand to welcome me.

"This is what it's like to work for a wire service. After a while you'll get used to it."

Griffin showed me around the office, introducing me to some of the staffers and explaining to me what my duties would be, including working on the racing desk with the tedious job of tearing results off one teletype machine from the eight or nine racetracks across the country, editing them mostly for punctuation, and then handing them to another teletype operator to punch them up and send out on the UPI wire to all their client newspapers. "We'll be sending you up to Yankee Stadium and to Shea Stadium to cover Yankees and Mets games, and there'll be press conferences around the city we'll want you to cover," Griffin said. "And once in a while," he lied, "you'll work on the racing desk over there."

I soon learned the racing desk—UN-5 as it was listed on Griffin's weekly assignment schedule—was primarily the province of the "last man hired" and I found myself spending two-to-three days a week on it. The only good thing about the racing desk was the hours. You reported to work at 1:00 PM and were usually done by 8:00 PM when the last races from the West Coast came in—perfect for a young, single guy in New York who could party late into the night and sleep in in the morning.

On one of my first days on the job at UPI, the day editor, a mousy soft-spoken man named Steve Smilanich, whom UPI had brought in from their Salt Lake City bureau to serve as Griffin's assistant, assigned me to cover a "Black is beautiful" press conference luncheon at Tavern on the Green. "Black is beautiful" was a cultural movement in the 1960s, celebrating people and styles connected to African heritage. At this particular press conference, Jackie Robinson was scheduled to be the featured speaker, which was why UPI sent a sports reporter to cover it. I got there early and observed an image I will never forget: a hunched over, white-haired man came limping from the adjoining sheep meadow across the restaurant parking lot. It took me a moment to realize it was Robinson.

A few minutes earlier, I had been introduced to Fred McMane, UPI's senior baseball writer who I would later learn was a lifelong Dodgers fan. "I'm not working today," McMane assured me. "I just wanted to come to this to see Jackie. I can't believe it. He's barely recognizable."

I accompanied McMane into the restaurant, where we immediately stopped at one of the minibars set up around the room where the event was to take place and ordered ourselves a couple of free gin and tonics. During the course of the luncheon, I had a few more drinks while dutifully filling up my notepad with the text of Robinson's remarks. It had been a highly enjoyable first UPI assignment—free food, free drinks, and meeting a legend in person—but as

I began heading to my car in the parking lot to head back to the office, McMane hollered to me: "Where you going?"

"I've got to go back to the office and write this story up," I said.

"Ahh, they don't care when you get back," McMane assured. "Let's go over and have a pop at Toots Shor's."

"Are you sure?" I asked.

"Oh yeah," McMane said, "there's no deadline on this story."

So we drove out of Tavern on the Green over to Toots Shor's saloon on West 51st Street where, lo and behold, there just happened to be a parking spot right in front of the place. McMane grabbed a couple seats at the huge circular bar and for the next couple of hours he gave me dissertation on UPI while plying me with more drinks. Then, suddenly, he glanced out the front door window and nudged me. "Uh, oh," he said, "it looks like they're towing your car away. That must not have been a legal parking spot."

Panicked, I rushed out the front door of Shor's to see my '67 Cutlass convertible up on a lift in the grips of a tow truck. "Stop! Stop!" I shouted. "That's my car!"

I later learned under New York State law tow truck operators are obligated to release the cars if the owner appears before they are able to tow them away. With a look of disgust on his face, the tow truck driver hit a release gear, and as I watched in horror, my Cutlass came crashing down from the hoist onto the pavement. Fortunately, there was no damage to the car, though I myself was severely impaired by the time I got back to the office.

"Where have you been all day?" Smilanich screamed.

"I was with Fred McMane," I said, realizing immediately that wasn't exactly a satisfactory explanation.

Smilanich was visibly angry. "You were supposed to come right back after the press conference," he said. "We need this story."

I tried to conceal my state of inebriation, but as I sat down bleary-eyed, I could barely make out the keys on my typewriter. Somehow I was eventually able to bang out a semi-coherent story, but as I learned later from the other staffers in the office, they had never seen Smilanich lose his temper like that. *Great*, I thought, *on my very first assignment for UPI, I managed to nearly get myself fired*. Nothing was ever said to McMane and I wasn't mad at him for leading me astray. We laughed about it for years after.

The next few weeks at UPI were fairly routine. Three days a week, I worked the racing desk. There were a couple of press conferences in the city from which I made certain to make a hasty retreat back to the office. On one occasion I was sent up to Yankee Stadium to cover a Yankees game and got my first introduction to Yankees manager Ralph Houk, who in a scrum of writers in the dugout went out of his way to spit tobacco juice all over my shoes. "That's Ralph's way with rookie writers he doesn't recognize," Phil Pepe of the *Daily News* told me. "He doesn't mean anything by it."

I guess I should've been glad for that, but my shoes were stained for life.

Come mid-July it was time for me to report back to South Carolina for two weeks of infantry training at Fort Gordon, Georgia, and I had no idea what fate was in store for me. As I left for the airport, I told my mother that if I didn't come back, she needed to make sure there was a full-scale investigation, which I'm sure must have been rather disconcerting to her.

Fort Gordon was 55,000 acres of mostly dense pines and swamps, a few miles southwest of Augusta, the home of The Masters. On the first day, my unit bivouacked deep into the woods and set up camp, where we slept in hammocks covered with mosquito netting. Each day we would take target practice in the mornings with our M-14 rifles, then embark on long hikes through the woods, presumably in search of imaginary Viet Cong hiding in the bushes, before returning to the camp at nightfall. I wasn't sure if it was a violation of Army regulations or merely standard-operating summer camp procedure for these National Guard units, but there was a goodly supply of beer on hand for the entire two weeks, and almost everyone in the unit had their bottles of hooch for nighttime imbibing.

As I crossed off the days, the two weeks went by without incident until the final night when our unit comrades began drinking early and getting more and more rambunctious. I looked at Paul, who I could see was sharing my sudden apprehension, and whispered: "I wonder if they're celebrating the end of camp—or the end of us?"

I didn't have to wait long. "Okay, you Yankee boys, step over here," hollered one of the sergeants, who was holding a pair of blindfolds, which he proceeded to affix on our heads. "Now strip! Everything! Right down to your skivvies!"

It was incessantly hot and humid, but at that point, I vividly remember shivering. I had no idea what was coming next other than it probably wasn't going to be good. I felt a tug on my shoulder, and then one of them was leading me to what felt like a soapbox they had set up in a clearing. "You boys know the words to 'Dixie'?" he asked.

"Uh...maybe...I think so," I replied.

"Well, good, you go first. Get on this soapbox and start singing!"

At that moment I felt forever grateful to my fifth-grade music teacher, who had taught us all the Southern songs and spirituals, and I slowly began crooning: "I wish I was in the land of cotton, old times there are not forgotten, look away, look away, look away Dixieland…"

But before I could go much further, they ripped the blindfolds off our heads, and as we stood there half naked, we found ourselves surrounded by a dozen or so figures in white robes and hoods, standing around a flaming cross. They were laughing diabolically, and now I was sure we were about to be sacrificed at the altar of the Grand Wizard. Instead, however, they reinstated our blindfolds and marched us back to camp. When the blindfolds were removed again, everyone was back in their fatigues, and it was as if nothing had ever happened.

The next day I flew home to New Jersey with both a tremendous sigh of relief that I was still alive and a very unsettling feeling in my stomach that, unbeknownst to me, for the last year I had apparently been enlisted in a chapter of the Ku Klux Klan. That last-day experience was horrifying. The South was a very different place in the '60s. The civil rights movement had not begun to reach fruition, and the Atlantic Coast Conference, of which South Carolina was a member— as well as the Southeastern and Southwest Conferences—were all still mostly segregated. In my senior year, 1969–70, when McGuire's Gamecocks were ACC champions with a 25–3 record, there were few Black basketball players in the ACC. Charlie Scott of North Carolina also happened to be the best player in the entire conference.

I remember something Hank Aaron, who grew up in Mobile, Alabama, told me when I interviewed him for my *1954* book. When he was in high school, Aaron said his favorite sport was football. "I was very good in football, and my mother hoped I could get a scholarship, but because Alabama and all the other big state schools were segregated, I wasn't going to go to college, which meant if I was going to pursue a professional sports career, it was going to have to be baseball. But if Alabama would have admitted Blacks, I might never have become a baseball player."

Imagine that.

CHAPTER THREE

"ALWAYS HAVE YOUR DIME, BILLY."

Milton Richman, the sports columnist and later sports editor at United Press International, was without doubt the strangest person I ever knew. A lifelong bachelor who grew up in a tiny, two-bedroom apartment in the Tremont Avenue section of the Bronx, where he slept in the same bed with his younger brother, Arthur, until they were both in their 40s, Milton was literally married to his "Today's Sport Parade" column at UPI. He once told me: "The reason I don't like sex, Billy, is because it gets you all sweaty and takes your mind off the column."

I suspected, too, Milton would never get married as long as his doting Jewish momma was alive. He and Arthur talked often with reverence about Clara Richman, and after she died, they enlisted a jeweler to make these garish gold rings with her face engraved on them, which they both wore proudly on their wedding ring fingers. In spring training of 1973, Milton and I were at Chicago White Sox camp in Sarasota, Florida, where the big story was the absence of Dick Allen, the defending American League MVP. As White Sox manager Chuck Tanner was lamely explaining to a group of reporters that Allen was delayed at home taking care of his mother,

I cringed as Milton thrust his finger with Clara Richman's "death mask" ring through the crowd and said somberly: "I can understand, Chuck. I know If my momma called me, I'd run home, too. She's always with me."

When Milton and Arthur were teenagers, they used to hang outside the visiting players' gate at Yankee Stadium getting autographs. They soon discovered the most accommodating players were the ones from the moribund, perennial last-place St. Louis Browns, who took such a liking to them they invited the two boys to stow away as "mascots" on the trains with them. Milton actually later played a year of minor league ball in the Browns' system before joining UPI as a full-fledged baseball writer. When I joined UPI, Milton was already the foremost baseball writer in the country, even though he was hardly a household name. "We are the 'swabbies' of the world, Billy," he told me, "wire service grunts who all the newspapers steal from and never give us bylines."

But as I soon discovered, Milton knew everybody in baseball—and I do mean everybody. On any given day at the office, I'd overhear him on the phone talking to the commissioner, an owner like George Steinbrenner or Bud Selig, or a prominent general manager like Gabe Paul of the Cleveland Indians or Jim Campbell of the Detroit Tigers. And at the ballpark, he had this bedside manner in his interviews with players that engendered instant trust. "They all want to tell me things, Billy," he was fond of saying, and they did.

Working for a wire service, where the motto was "deadline every minute" (as it later became the case for everyone in the age of Twitter), we oftentimes didn't have the luxury of going back to an office and typing a story up. Instead, for the sake of expediency, the vast majority of our stories had to be dictated by phone to an editor in New York and put immediately on the wire to all the client newspapers.

I used to say baseball held its annual winter meetings on Milton's behalf because there was nary a trade that he didn't break. I loved watching him in action. Whenever there would be an announcement of a forthcoming trade posted on the press room bulletin board, Milton would scurry out of the room and come back a few minutes later and say to me: "Okay, Billy, these are the players in the deal. Go write up the story, dictate it to the office, and instruct them to hold on to it until I tell them."

That was exactly what happened at the 1974 winter meetings in New Orleans when the Montreal Expos traded perennial All-Star center fielder Willie Davis to the Texas Rangers for reliever Don Stanhouse and infielder Pete Mackanin. Milton had gotten the deal from Expos general manager Jim Fanning and, as soon as the parties from the two teams came into the press room, he walked up to the podium and whispered something to Fanning. Then, turning to me on the open phone to UPI in New York, he hollered: "Okay, Billy. Let it go!"

With that Hal Bock, the Associated Press' lead writer at the meetings, threw up his hands and shouted: "That's it! That does it! I've have enough of this shit!" and stormed out of the press room across the lobby and into a private cocktail reception hosted by a group from Toronto seeking an expansion franchise. Bock was an avowed teetotaler, but at that moment, he was so infuriated he couldn't see straight and went up to the bar and ordered a double martini, which he then proceeded to drain in three gulps. Even though they were our competitors, I often actually felt sorry for the poor "swabbies" from the AP who, at least at the baseball winter meetings, had become resigned to being the Washington Generals to Milton's Harlem Globetrotters. Bock was an excellent baseball writer and a good sport as well, and whenever we would cross paths at various baseball events, he would whisper in my ear, "Let it go, Billy."

For their part, however, the AP did have their own very worthy equivalent to Milton in Will Grimsley, their main lead writer for all the major sports events, especially golf, tennis, horse racing, and the Olympics. Grimsley, who mostly stayed away from baseball during the season, had a special knack for embellishment and catchy leads that routinely set him apart from the other wire service writers of the day. At UPI we referred to him as the "Grim Reaper," and none of us relished going up against him at a big event.

Fred Down, the baseball editor at UPI and another valued mentor to me who'd covered the New York Yankees for *The New York Sun* in the late '40s, loved regaling us with Grimsley stories, particularly the one about the 1960 Summer Olympics in Rome when Grimsley was going up against UPI sports editor Leo H. Peterson. The highlight of those Olympics was the marathon in which an Ethiopian named Abebe Bikila became the first in his country to win a gold medal. Not long after Bakila crossed the finish line, Peterson filed a colorfully descriptive lead, "Abebe Bikila, the sweat streaming down his face from the blistering Rome heat, became the first Ethiopian countryman to win an Olympic gold medal, winning the marathon in a world record time of 2:15.16." Out it went to all the UPI clients.

But a while later, as Down recounted, the UPI sports desk in New York received a call from an editor at *The New York Times*, saying that in Grimsley's Associated Press story, Bikila was reported to not be wearing any shoes. When this was relayed to Peterson over in Rome, he shot back: "That's bullshit. I was right there. The guy was wearing shoes!"

But then, about an hour later, *The Times* editor called again and said that the AP had just filed their "first lead" on the marathon story—this one with quotes—and still maintained that Bikila was not wearing shoes. When this was now reported to Peterson, he responded angrily: "Same old Grimsley. Making shit up. Pictures will bare us out."

At this point the befuddled editors on the UPI sports desk felt compelled to relate the dispute to UPI editor Roger Tatarian who said: "Call me when the pictures come in."

It didn't take long before the first pictures from Rome began rolling off the telegraph machine, and there he was, Abibe Bikila in all his barefooted splendor, crossing the finish line at the marathon. When Tatarian, a man of notoriously few words, saw the picture, he sat down at the desk himself and fired off the following missive to Peterson: "Peterson. Pictures have arrived. No shoes. Tatarian."

Flash forward 13 years to the 1973 World University Games in Moscow, where I found myself with the unenviable task of going up against the Grim Reaper. Besides baseball, I was also UPI's main track and field writer, and UPI had given me this assignment to go to Moscow to cover these games in preparation for covering the 1976 Olympics in Montreal. I had no idea how to cover a multifaceted event like this and for the first week I was getting slaughtered by Grimsley, while wasting valuable time by running around to each venue to see the competition firsthand. Once I realized that, as the main lead writer, all I had to do was sit in the office and compile all the stories coming in from the other reporters at the various venues and compose one comprehensive sum-up of the events of the day, I was starting to feel good about myself in this first major assignment at UPI. I felt I was at least holding my own against Grimsley, when one night I had a message from Down in New York: "ROX [which was our term for the AP, though no one could explain why despite my repeated inquires] reporting of fight in the balcony of the Israel–Cuba basketball game tonight in which the Israeli flag was torn. How please?"

I immediately called our basketball correspondent about the report, and he insisted it didn't happen. "I was at the game," he said. "And if something like that had gone on, I'm sure I would have seen it."

So I dutifully messaged Down back: "Our guy insists there was no fight. Sounds like another Grimsley exaggeration."

But the following morning, I came into the Moscow bureau office and found a copy of *The New York Times* left on my desk. On the front page was a huge picture of two people tearing up an Israeli flag in the balcony of the gymnasium where the Israel–Cuba game was going on. My heart sank. It sank even further when I looked at the teletype machine and saw the message from Down in New York: "Sorry, Billy. Pictures have arrived. Flag torn."

As UPI's only sports columnist, Milton was obligated to cover all the major sports events, but his one love was baseball, and he went out of his way to write about baseball during the winter months. He had no interest in basketball, hockey, or college football and dreaded going to the Super Bowl. In 1976 the Super Bowl was played in Miami, and Milton arranged to get me a press pass for the game. The night before the game, I was sitting in the press room watching Joe Carnicelli, UPI's pro football writer, feverishly typing his night lead on deadline when Milton came racing up to him, shouting: "Joey, I got it! I got it."

Stopping his typing, Carnicelli turned around and asked somewhat exasperatedly: "What is it, Milton?"

"I got it, Joey," Milton repeated.

"What, Milton?" Carnicelli said.

Then, leaning down and whispering in Carnicelli's ear, Milton pronounced: "Dick Drago to the Angels."

You had to understand. To Milton the trade of a marginal relief pitcher the first week of January was a far bigger "stop the presses" story than the Super Bowl, especially when Milton had it alone.

As much as Milton continued to amuse me with his nuttiness, I also learned so much from him. Whenever we were on the road together, he always made sure to introduce me as "my associate Billy Madden" to everyone in baseball at the ballparks, World Series, All-Star galas, and restaurants. Milton loved making introductions. Consequently, when I went to the *Daily News* in 1978, I had as many or more contacts than any of their baseball writers because of Milton.

One of the people Milton introduced me to was Steinbrenner. It was during the 1976 season, and the Yankees were in pursuit of their first American League pennant in 12 years. I told Milton I'd like to interview Steinbrenner, and he arranged for me to go up to Yankee Stadium for a one-on-one with the Yankee boss. With some trepidation I walked into Steinbrenner's office only to quickly be put at ease by his initial warm and friendly presence. During the interview, however, Steinbrenner began launching into a fusillade of sharp criticism of his fellow owners, league officials, and the state of umpiring. At one point he referred to National League president Chub Feeney as a "useless fop"—a term I had never heard before and had to look up in the dictionary when I got back to the office.

I didn't use the Feeney "fop" slur in my story, but I did quote a lot of the rest of Steinbrenner's complaints. My story had been out on the wire only a couple of hours when Milton called me at home, quite upset. "Steinbrenner's really pissed," he said. "He says you quoted him saying a lot of bad stuff about other people in baseball he says he never said. He wants a retraction."

"But Milton," I protested. "I have it all here in my notes. I didn't misquote him. I don't know what to tell you."

"Well, you're going to have to go back up to the stadium and explain that to him," Milton said. "At the very least, you're gonna have to apologize."

Grudgingly, I went back up to Yankee Stadium to meet with Steinbrenner again, and this time his mood was devoid of any pleasantries. "I have to tell you, young man, I am not happy with that story you wrote," he said. "Most of that stuff I told you was off the record. I was just trying to help you understand a lot of the people in baseball. You obviously need to learn about journalism. So for the time being, I'm not going to talk to you anymore. You have to learn to be more responsible. I only did this interview as a favor to Milt Richman and until I feel I can trust you I won't be talking to you."

It was not the last time Steinbrenner would put me in his penalty box.

A couple of years earlier, Milton had assigned me to have lunch with broadcaster Shelby Whitfield, the former radio voice of the Washington Senators who was in New York promoting his book, *Kiss It Goodbye*, a scathing indictment of Texas Rangers owner Bob Short's underhanded move of the team from Washington to Dallas-Fort Worth after the 1971 season. At the end of my interview with Whitfield, he thanked me and then said: "By the way are you aware of the Tony Horton story?"

It was in reference to the Cleveland Indians slugging first baseman who went on the disabled list for what was termed "exhaustion" in late August 1970 and never returned.

"Only that he was in the peak of his career and retired for no reason," I said.

"That wasn't it," Whitfield said. "It's much deeper than that. It's a good story for you that's never been written. Talk to Alvin Dark, who was the Indians manager, and talk to Ken Harrelson, Horton's teammate. I'm telling you: it's a big story that baseball's covering up."

When I got back to the office, I told Milton what Whitfield had said to me about Tony Horton, and he abruptly cut me off. "Stay away from that, Billy," Milton said. "That's not a story we want to get into."

I have to say I was a bit stunned at Milton's reaction. He was such a bloodhound for big stories and yet he was so adamant about not wanting me to look into what happened to Horton. I never brought it up again with him, but it was something that stayed in the back of my mind long after I left UPI for the *Daily News* as the Yankees beat writer. Finally, on June of 1997, I decided to look into it after having lunch in the Yankee Stadium press room with Mike Paul, a Texas scout who'd been Horton's roommate with the Indians.

I later discovered Horton's troubles in 1970 began in spring training when he staged a long salary holdout, incurring the wrath of the Indians' fans. At one point, Dark, who was both the Indians' manager and general manager, told him if he didn't sign what Cleveland was offering him, they were prepared to move Ken Harrelson from left field to first base. Horton grudgingly relented and signed for the Indians' offer of $45,000, and the next day, Harrelson broke his ankle sliding into third base. Horton never got over it and brooded the entire season, slowly breaking down mentally. Yankees third baseman Graig Nettles, who was Horton's teammate on the Indians in 1970, told me: "Tony was a stud, as good a hitter as I ever saw, but then one day he just went crazy, wandering around the clubhouse aimlessly during a game with just a towel and slippers."

Many of the Indians players, including Horton, stayed at a little motel called the Blue Grass on the outskirts of Cleveland, and I was able to track down the motel's proprietor, Larry Mako, who provided me with the biggest piece of the puzzle. "One night I got a call from one of our security people who'd found Tony sitting in his car in the parking lot with both his wrists slit and bleeding profusely," Mako said. "They rushed him to the hospital, and the next day, his father and the Indians officials came by and cleaned out his room. We never saw him again."

Sam McDowell, the Indians' 20-game winning ace pitcher in 1970 who later went on to become a drug and alcohol counselor for baseball, explained to me that Horton, who was only 25, was deeply troubled and could no longer play baseball. "From what I understand," McDowell said, "the doctors told him he had to completely divorce himself from baseball. He was so high strung with such a drive to succeed, and when he wasn't, it set him off. It affected him every time he saw his fellow teammates or had any kind of connection with baseball."

Now I knew why Milton didn't want me to pursue whatever had happened to Horton. I'm sure he knew about the suicide attempt and felt it was better not to reveal it.

Milton was full of eccentricities, not the least of which was his obsession with his physical fitness. Short and stocky, and then in his early 50s, he bragged that he'd been the fastest player in the Browns' system, and to prove it he would, unprompted, launch into a sprint down the hallway outside the UPI offices or across hotel lobbies. On other occasions we'd be checking into a hotel, and Milton would say: "I bet you don't know anyone who can do 20 one-armed pushups," and before I could answer, he'd hand me his sports jacket, drop to the floor, and begin pumping off a dozen one-armed pushups in front of the startled lobby crowd.

It was at the 1974 winter baseball meetings in New Orleans, however, that I earned Milton's eternal respect—not for a story I broke but for beating him in footrace. We were at a bar on Bourbon Street in the wee hours of the morning, and Milton, who was not a big drinker, had nevertheless had one tequila too many and was feeling his oats. For whatever reason, he'd always been fascinated by the fact that I'd been a state champion sprinter in high school and he wanted me to prove it. "I'll bet I can beat you in a 50-yard dash, right here, Billy," he said.

"What are we betting?" I asked.

"Fifty bucks," Milton said.

"Okay," I said, "Fifty bucks."

We walked out of the bar onto Bourbon Street, which was still fairly crowded at 2:00 AM, and Milton pointed to another bar that looked to be about 50 yards away. "From here to there," he said. "I'll count it off."

We then proceeded to get down on one knee, as if in imaginary starting blocks, and as Milton counted off, "on your mark, set, go," I burst out in front of him and kept running until I reached the other bar. When I looked back, Milton was still at the starting line.

"I have to admit," he said. "You are really fast, Billy. I never saw anyone so quick out of the starting blocks." With that he peeled off five $10 bills and handed them to me.

For the rest of my time at UPI, Milton would tell people in baseball I was the only person who ever beat him in a race, and I never dared to counter that it was no great feat beating a middle-aged man who'd had too much to drink. But even though I may have impressed Milton with my speed, he was always quick to remind me I was still a novice. The following October, Milton included me on the UPI team covering the 1975 World Series between the Boston Red Sox and Cincinnati Reds, which turned out to be one of the greatest Fall Classics of all time, particularly the iconic 12-inning Game Six that was decided by Carlton Fisk's home run at 12:34 AM that ricocheted off the Fenway Park left-field foul pole. Before the game Milton had divvied up assignments to our four writers, mine being the losers' clubhouse after the game.

As soon I saw as Fisk's ball land safely, as Fenway Park erupted in unrestrained euphoria, I made a mad dash out of the press box to the elevator and felt Milton grab me by the shoulder. "Billy," he said somberly, "don't fuck up down there."

With those reassuring words still ringing in my ears, I was at the front of the line heading into the losing Reds' clubhouse, fully expecting a funereal mood after this crushing defeat that had forced a Game Seven. Instead, the first person I encountered was Pete Rose, standing atop a trainer's table in the middle of the room, extolling to all what a tremendous game we had all just witnessed. "You guys believe what a great game that was?" Rose screamed. "In the eighth inning, I went over to [Red Sox shortstop Rick] Burleson and said: 'Do you believe this game? This is the most exciting game I've ever played in!'"

As I was feverishly scribbling down Rose's unrestrained, jubilant assessment of the game, I had a momentary flash of panic. "Oh my god," I thought, "I fucked up! Did I go to the wrong clubhouse?"

Two months later at the 1975 winter meetings at the Diplomat Hotel in Hollywood, Florida, however, I really did earn Milton's admiration for breaking a story. For the first three days of the meetings, trade activity was at a standstill due to the nagging No. 1 issue on the agenda—the American League owners' decision whether to re-admit Bill Veeck back into their lodge. Veeck was the all-time baseball maverick whose previous stints as owner of the Indians, Browns, and White Sox were marked with wild publicity stunts that continuously ruffled the feathers of his fellow baseball lords. In 1976 the White Sox were teetering on the verge of bankruptcy, and Veeck, who had sold the team in 1961, was now seeking to buy it back despite the perception of being grossly underfinanced. In fact, a couple of weeks earlier, the AL owners had told him he could not be approved until he added more investors and re-adjusted his financial package.

On the third day of the meetings, I was sitting on the floor of a hallway off the main lobby of the Diplomat, reading a newspaper to pass away the boredom while leaning against what I thought was a wall but was in fact a partition concealing a private meeting room. Suddenly, I could hear raised voices from the other side of the partition, particularly one voice that grew louder and louder, which I later came to realize was that of John Fetzer, the highly respected owner of the Detroit Tigers: "Gentlemen, I've been in the league for 20 years and over that time I've seen one slipshod thing after another. We rush in here to vote and then rush out to get drinks. We've done more soul-searching on this deal than at any time before, and now that it has been set, we have left these people over a barrel. We told them: get more investors and their finances firmed up, and they did it. We've got to be men about this. I don't like it any more than you do, allowing a guy in here who's called me a son of a bitch over and over. But gentlemen, we've got to take another vote."

As I hurriedly wrote down Fetzer's admonishment of his fellow owners, all I could think was: "Holy shit! They voted Veeck down!"

I ran into the pressroom and told Milton what I'd heard, showing him my notes, and together we commandeered a phone booth off the lobby where Milton dictated my story to the office—at the same time the American League owners were taking a second vote to approve Veeck as owner of the White Sox. By the time they came out of their meeting, the whole story was out on the UPI wire, including Fetzer's quotes, and the previously quiet 1975 winter meetings had turned into a shitstorm. Particularly outraged was Bob Fishel, the vice president of public relations for the American League, who the next day came into the meeting of the Baseball Writers Association and demanded that I be kicked out of the association or at the very least be severely sanctioned for improperly eavesdropping on a private meeting.

The following spring I felt gratified when Veeck—in a first-person piece for *Sports Illustrated* on his return to baseball—wrote: "The only reason the vote got out while they were meeting was that a kid named Bill Madden, who worked for Milt Richman at UPI, slipped into the anteroom and pressed his ear to the wall just in time to hear the result."

Besides Milton's alleged running prowess and his physical fitness, something else he took great pride in relating was that in 30-some odd years at UPI he'd missed only one day of work, which he attributed to exhaustion due to a night of too much sex. (I often wondered if he'd had regret in taking his mind off the column for an entire night.) Once in the UPI office men's room, Milton became engaged in a conversation with one of our newer writers, Fred Lief, who himself had missed work the previous day to attend a funeral. "You know you can't bring back the dead," Milton said sternly.

"I guess so," Lief replied, choosing not to get into a debate with his boss about missing a day of work.

"But then, Freddie," Milton added with a wan smile, "how do you know *I'm* not Jesus?"

In Boston one time, Milton spotted a McDonald's around the corner from Fenway Park where we were headed and asked me and a friend if we wanted a hamburger—whereupon he went up to the young lady behind the window and introduced himself as the "sports editor and sports columnist for United Press International and my two associates here, and we would like three hamburgers, but I would like mine medium rare."

Milton's best friend was Frank Lane, the legendary former general manager of the White Sox, St. Louis Cardinals, and Indians in the '40s and '50s. Lane himself was one of the great characters of baseball. Nicknamed "Trader," he made more than 400 deals involving nearly 700 players in his day. In 1960, while with Cleveland, he even traded managers, sending his man, Joe Gordon, to the Tigers for Jimmy Dykes. Over the winters Milton and Lane vacationed together in Acapulco, Mexico, and later Lane would join him in spring training in Tampa, Florida.

Lane was in his early 80s then and working as a top scout for Harry Dalton, the general manager of the Angels.

He could barely see but was too vain to wear glasses, a defect that would ordinarily inhibit his ability to scout players. But Dalton didn't care about that. He hired Frank to sit with the scouts at all the games, pick their brains, and gather intelligence, which he would also pass on to Milton.

My job was to drive the two of them around to all the camps, and I have to say it was the one of the most enjoyable—not to mention educational—experiences of my life, listening to these two baseball lifers telling stories about old baseball players and arguing with each other about everything. Even though Lane had had a remarkable career—in the early '50s he turned the White Sox from American League doormats to perennial contenders with a string of lopsided trades for future Hall of Famers Nellie Fox and Minnie Minoso and seven-time All-Star lefty Billy Pierce—Milton loved needling him about the worst trade he ever made. In 1956, when Lane was with the Cardinals, he traded their Rookie of the Year centerfielder Bill Virdon to the Pittsburgh Pirates for another short, squat center fielder named Bobby De Greco, who hit .217 that year.

One night we were having dinner in a cheap Italian restaurant—a red sauce joint with linoleum floors and a little bar in the front with a cash register and a revolving dessert tray enclosed with a clear plastic cover—on the outskirts of Tampa. After spending much of the night arguing over who had a better life story for a book, Milton asked Lane if he wanted any dessert.

"Well, yes," Lane said, pointing to the revolving dessert tray on the counter. "I'm gonna have some of that flam up there."

"I beg your pardon, Frankie," Milton said. "But it's pronounced flon."

"Now goddammit, Milton," Lane shot back. "I've been eating that all my life, and it's called flam!"

"Frankie," Milton said, "it's flon!"

"Dammit, Milton, it's flam!"

Finally, Milton summoned the waitress, a young girl who looked to be still in her teens, over to our table.

"Good evening, ma'am," Milton said. "My name is Milton Richman, and I'm the sports editor and sports columnist for United Press International, and here with me is my associate Billy Madden, and Frank Lane, the former general manager of the Chicago White Sox, St. Louis Cardinals, and Cleveland Indians. Now, ma'am, we need you to settle a little dispute here. Do you see that dessert spinning around on the tray up on the counter there?"

The waitress turned and glanced at the counter.

"Well, ma'am," Milton continued, "do you pronounce that dessert flam or flon?"

For a brief second, the waitress looked a little perplexed before answering: "Well, I don't know, sir. I always thought that was caramel custard!"

That was one of the few times I ever saw Milton truly flummoxed.

By the late '70s, free agency in baseball was becoming a driving force for the players and along with it came the rise of the player agents, whom Milton detested, but the other writers began cultivating. More often than not, the biggest deals at the winter meetings were now free-agent signings rather than trades, where Milton invariably had his sources from both clubs.

At the 1978 winter meetings in Orlando, Florida, the overriding storyline was the free agency of Pete Rose, who at 37 was already one of baseball's all-time ambassadors and ninth on the all-time hits list with 3,164 after 16 sterling seasons with the Reds. For spring training Milton always had a UPI base in Tampa, which was also the training home of the Reds. As a result, Milton had a particularly close relationship with the Reds front office, their manager Sparky Anderson, and their star players Rose; Johnny Bench; Tony Perez; and Joe Morgan.

Rose had left his hometown team with his sights set on becoming the highest-paid player in baseball (which he would achieve with a four-year, $3.225 million deal), and

Milton was determined to be the one to break the story of his signing—so determined that in one of the wildest days of the winter meetings he reported Rose signing first with the Kansas City Royals and then the Atlanta Braves before finally getting it right with the Philadelphia Phillies. I felt bad for him as all the other writers at the meetings were ridiculing him for his mad scrambling on the Rose signing. But at the press conference later in the day, Rose, holding aloft his new Phillies jersey, shouted out to the assembled media: "You guys gotta give credit to Milt Richman. He's the guy who broke the story!" Milton, standing off to the side, beamed with pride.

On June 9, 1986, Milton Richman was found dead in his apartment in New York's Greenwich Village. The victim of a heart attack, he was only 64. In the years following, as the baseball writing profession changed dramatically with the intrusion of social media and the decline of newspapers, I thought of him often and wondered how he would survive in the age of cellphones and the internet. One of the first things he instructed me when I came to UPI was to "always have your dime" because a large majority of our stories were dictated from pay phone booths.

I especially thought of Milton one late night at the 2014 winter meetings in San Diego where the big story was the free agency of perennial All-Star lefty Jon Lester. Earlier in the day word had come down that Lester had narrowed his choice to the San Francisco Giants, Red Sox, and Chicago Cubs, and then it was reported that the Giants had dropped out. It was nearly 10:00 PM Pacific Coast Time, and I had just come from dinner with Hal Bodley of MLB.com to find the press room mostly empty except for small contingents of writers from Boston and Chicago. As Bodley and I were checking out the bulletin board for the announcements of the day, some guy poked his head in the door at the rear of the press room and shouted: "Rosenthal just tweeted. It's the Cubs!"

With that there was a scurry of the Boston and Chicago writers, dashing out of the press room on their cellphones. Once Milton ruled the world at these meetings with his dogged reporting and fountain of sources, but by this time, Kenny Rosenthal, first of FOX Sports and then The Athletic, had established himself as the supreme breaker of baseball news with multiple agent and players union sources not to mention the MLB hierarchy itself. "So this is what our business has come to," I said to Bodley. "Now everyone sits around and waits for the Rosenthal tweet."

CHAPTER FOUR

COPS, BOOBS, AND THE YANKEES

UPI was located on the 12th floor of the *Daily News* building at 220 East 42nd Street, and as a result, I saw a lot of the *Daily News* sportswriters during my time there, in particular Dick Young, the legendary *Daily News* sports columnist, who took a liking to me and was amused by my stories about Milton Richman and his eccentricities. He'd also seen me at work with Richman at the winter meetings, spring training, and the World Series. In his later years, Young was most identifiable by his flowing mane of white hair, which got me to give him a nickname—"The Great White Poobah"—a moniker that stuck within the local writers' corps.

In 1978 at Young's urging, the *Daily News* agreed to promote Phil Pepe from New York Yankees beat writer to a general sports columnist, and it was also Young's recommendation to sports editor Buddy Martin that they hire me to cover the Yankees. In my first meeting with Martin, we went to the Lantern Coffee Shop across the street from the *Daily News*, and he said to me: "I can't emphasize enough how important this beat is that I'm hiring you for. There are three things that sell this newspaper—cops, boobs, and the

Yankees. The prototypical *Daily News* has cops, crime, and mayhem on the front page; semi-naked pop tarts on the gossip pages inside; and Steinbrenner, Reggie Jackson, and Billy Martin all going at it on the back page. Steinbrenner thinks he owns the back page of the tabloids in this town, and the fact is he probably does."

I never forgot that.

At the time of that interview with Martin, the New York newspapers were all about to go on strike—a strike that lasted nearly four months and through the '78 World Series—and my hiring was delayed until November. Pepe's promotion was put off until 1980, and so in 1979, I shared the Yankees beat with him, including the coverage of Thurman Munson's death in which Pepe flew to Canton, Ohio, with the team for the funeral, and I covered the first game back at Yankee Stadium along with Steve Goldstein, our investigative sports reporter. To this day it remains about the most dramatic game I ever covered. Our lead on the back page of the *Daily News* was all-encompassing of the emotional scene that engulfed the stadium that night, much of it orchestrated by George Steinbrenner: "The last words of America the Beautiful had barely left Robert Merrill's throat when the applause began. It went on for an incredible eight minutes, falling and rising to a crescendo, the sellout Yankee Stadium crowd refusing to leave its feet and allow the game to begin. The Yankee players stood, heads bowed, motionless on the field, fresh black armbands on their sleeves. A picture of their beloved captain flashed on the scoreboard. No catcher stood behind home plate, the ground symbolically empty. One's eye was drawn to a white banner, etched in black, hanging from the upper deck in right that said simply: '15 Thanks.' If you were human, if the power to reason was yours, you could not help but be moved by this moment."

Years later, Jerry Murphy, a special front-office assistant at the time, relayed to me how Steinbrenner, upon being informed of the plane crash, summoned all the Yankees front-office people into his office and barked instructions to them as to how he wanted things handled at the stadium: the black arm bands, Munson's locker being cleared out forever except for his catching gear with just the No. 15 affixed overhead where his nameplate had been, the vacating of home plate before the game, and a message to appear on the center-field scoreboard, which Steinbrenner himself wrote: "Our captain and leader has not left us—today, tomorrow, this year, next … Our endeavors will reflect our love and admiration for him."

"George had been crying when we first went into his office, his head slumped in his arms, and then he suddenly snapped back to reality and went into his full George Patton mode, giving us all our marching orders," Murphy said. "It was therapeutic for him. No one had to time to think about this horrible event, and George was strong for all of us. In my opinion, it was his finest hour."

The entire 1979 season was a disaster. The Yankees never recovered from Munson's death or the thumb injury to Goose Gossage suffered in a shower room fight with teammate Cliff Johnson that sidelined the Yankees closer for weeks. Over the winter Billy Martin was fired as Yankees manager for the second time and Gene "The Stick" Michael took over as general manager, making sweeping changes to the roster and hiring former Yankees third-base coach Dick Howser as manager. I was really looking forward to my first spring training as the Yankees beat writer when Buddy Martin threw up an unexpected roadblock at me. "I know you can't wait to get to Fort Lauderdale," he said, "but it's gonna have to wait a couple of weeks because I want you to go with me to the Winter Olympics in Lake Placid."

"The Winter Olympics?" I protested. "C'mon, Buddy, I don't know anything about skiing and bobsledding. What am I gonna do up there?"

"No, no, no I need you with me 'Mad Dog'," he said, calling me by a nickname he bestowed upon me. "You're gonna love it. It'll be a great experience, and the Yankees will still be there when the Olympics are over."

As it was, the *Daily News* spent a small fortune on our Winter Olympics coverage, renting four apartments right in town within walking distance to most of the venues and outfitting our team of eight reporters with heavy red down parkas with the *Daily News* logo on them and insulated furry boots. And as I learned when he showed up at my house in New Jersey, they had also supplied Buddy with a spanking new SUV for the drive to and from Lake Placid.

For the first week and a half, I did a bunch of small features on cross-country skiers, bobsledders, and a story Buddy especially liked, which the *News* headlined "The Daring Young Men in Their Flying Machines" about a group of ski jumpers called "forerunners" whose job it was to prepare the surface of the ski jump by making repeated dangerous 70-meter jumps into the soft, deep, snowy landing below.

On Friday night, February 22, Buddy and I were at the apartment working on separate stories for the Sunday paper while monitoring the U.S.–Soviet Union hockey game, which was only available on closed circuit TV in Lake Placid. Nobody expected the all-amateur Americans to even make a game of it against the mighty Russians, a team of professionals, which a year earlier had routed a team of National Hockey League All Stars 6–0. But when the game reached the third period, the Americans were only trailing 3-2, and we both stopped writing. "This is starting to look like it may be a very big story, Mad Dog," Buddy said.

And then when the Americans' Mark Johnson fired a shot under the Russian goalie's outstretched glove to tie the game at the 8:39-minute mark, Buddy burst from his chair, grabbed his clunky Texas Instruments computer, and started out the door. "I'm heading up to the arena, Mad Dog," he said, "to start coordinating the coverage."

"What do you want me to do?" I asked.

"Oh, you'll come up with something," he said. "I gotta go."

A couple of minutes later when Mike Eruzione scored the go-ahead goal for Team USA, I grabbed my jacket, pulled on my boots, and ventured out into the Lake Placid night. Main Street was empty and desolate save for some faraway lights at the very end. As I trudged my way through the snow, I could hear music coming from the building with the lights. *Great*, I said to myself, *A bar. People to talk to about the game.*

But it was not just a bar. It was, of all things, an American Legion hall, and the people shouting and celebrating inside were a bunch of World War II veterans. The moment I walked in the door, I was grabbed by this craggy-face man wearing an old beat-up Army hat and clutching a small American flag in one hand. "Here," he said. "Take this flag! Tonight is a night we are all proud to be Americans."

His name, I learned, was Henry James Miller, and he had tears in his eyes as he joined in the "U-S-A" chants filling the hall. "This morning," Miller said, "I got down on my knees and said: 'Dear God, lead our nation to regain the way of life that was established long ago when people gave up their lives for something they believed in.' I cried then and I'm crying here again tonight because our young team did something out there no team on Earth could ever have done. They brought to life the conscience of our nation."

As I scribbled down Miller's words in my notebook, another vet handed me a glass of scotch. "Drink up my friend," he said. "Celebrate America! We're No. 1!"

What incredible fortune! I thought. *An American Legion hall in the middle of Lake Placid on the night the American hockey team pulled off the greatest upset in the history of sports!*

I threw down my scotch, ran out the door, and headed for the arena to find Buddy. There were no cell phones then and no way to tell him I had indeed found something. When I got to the arena, Buddy was in a small auxiliary press room, divvying out assignments to our other reporters at the game when I told him where I'd been and read off my notes to him. "Oh, man" Buddy said, "this is great shit!"

He immediately began typing a story on his TI. He then grabbed one of the phones and called the *Daily News* night editor. "We've got a really big developing story up here," he said.

"What's that?" the night editor said, totally unaware of the hockey game.

"This is one of the biggest stories in the history of sports!" Buddy exclaimed. "You're gonna want it on Page One."

"I don't know," the editor said, "we're planning on leading the paper with the rise in inflation."

This was a prime example of why when we in sports came up with a really big story we dreaded the editor in chief saying "we're taking this up front." Because inevitably the final product after being homogenized by the city or metro desk was unrecognizable from the original copy by the time it got in the paper and it often ended up on page three or four rather than page one. I had that happen to me on a number of occasions as the Steinbrenner Yankees were constantly making tabloid front page-worthy news, and whenever it did, I recited the famous words of Stanley Woodward, the legendary sports editor of the old *New York Herald Tribune*, the day Dodgers manager Leo Durocher switched teams to the archrival Giants in 1948. Told by the editor in chief they were taking the Durocher story up front, Woodward snapped: "Why in the world would you ever want to take a story like this, the biggest sports story in New York history, and *bury* it on Page One?"

Fortunately, no one up front did much tinkering with Buddy's and my story, and they placed it on page three. But the front page of the *Daily News* the next day—a big, bold headline **INFLATION RATE JUMPS TO 18%**—dwarfing a small sub headline "U.S. beats Russia in hockey" merely confirmed ours—and Woodward's—worst fear. The *Daily News* had managed to bury the biggest sports upset of all time on page three.

This was also why I was most grateful to depart the cold and snow of Lake Placid, out of the daily potential grasp of news side, and on to Fort Lauderdale, Florida, for my rookie season as the Yankees beat man and their new manager, Howser. Though the Yankees won 103 games in 1980, it proved to be a constant tug of war between Howser and Steinbrenner and never a dull moment for the beat writers. Whenever I had filled in for Pepe in 1979, he counseled me: "Don't worry about your early story [which was used to hold space in the first editions of the paper until the game]. The Yankees will always provide."

And how they did. I'd walk into the Yankees clubhouse before the games, and they'd all be sitting there in front of their lockers anxious to vent about one thing or another—be it playing time or Steinbrenner. Reggie Jackson would practically stick his foot out as you passed his locker. It was why they called it the Bronx Zoo. As the season went on, I kept remembering Richman's famous words: "They all want to tell me things."

(By contrast, today all the new stadiums in baseball have built-in clubhouses within the clubhouses where the players all hang out free of the intrusions of the media. Even though the writers are still accorded an hour in the clubhouse before each game, it's basically a waste of time as most of the players' lockers are empty, and the writers wind up talking to each other.)

Throughout the 1980 season, Bobby Murcer, in particular, had been complaining about being platooned by Howser. Murcer was one of Steinbrenner's favorites and had The Boss' support in his running feud with Howser. Prior to a Yankees road trip to Seattle, a story leaked out that Steinbrenner thought it might be a good idea for Howser to try Murcer at first base. This set off one of the wildest days in the history of being a Yankees beat writer.

When we arrived at the Kingdome prior to the first game in Seattle, Howser was sitting in the dugout, and a half-open brown box with a first baseman's glove sat next to him with a visible postage mark "Bronx, New York." When we asked him who the glove was for, Howser just smiled. "I don't know," he said.

"Are you planning on using Murcer at first base?" we pressed.

"Not that I know of," Howser replied.

As it turned out, that was the last anyone saw of the mysterious first baseman's glove, but the Yankees had provided the beat writers with their "early"—or at least the first of many earlies that day.

For when we got upstairs to the press box, there came word that Ron Guidry was volunteering to go to the bullpen while Gossage was recovering from a minor arm injury. This was far bigger news than a phony story of Murcer playing first base. Looking down on the field, we could see Guidry long-tossing with some of the other pitchers in left field, so we ran back down to try and confirm this report. In one of the more unconventional interviews I could ever remember, we shouted questions to Guidry from 100 feet away, eliciting mostly smiles and one-word answers. Meanwhile, at the same time, Jim Spencer, the Yankees' left-handed platoon first baseman, emerged out of nowhere. "I have an announcement to make," Spencer said.

"Just a minute, Jim," I said. "We're trying to talk to Guidry here."

"I'm sorry," Spencer said, "but this is important. I have a statement to make."

"Okay," I said impatiently. "What is it, Jim?"

With that Spencer pulled out a piece of paper and began reading: "I just want to make it very clear that I resent the idea that Bobby Murcer should be a first baseman here. I have been a first baseman my entire career and won Gold Gloves, and now they're talking about replacing me with someone who's never even played the position? I find that insulting and I'm not going to accept this."

So in addition to the Guidry volunteering for the bullpen story, we had another chapter to the Murcer to first-base nonsense and we rushed back up to the press box to begin trying to put all these earlies into one concise story that by now was probably going to take precedence over the game that night. But just as we began typing away, suddenly "Chicken" Stanley, the Yankees' popular veteran utility infielder, appeared in the press box in full uniform. "I need your attention, guys," Stanley said, "I just want you to know that I have demanded a trade. I'm tired of sitting on the bench and I'm at the point of my career where I need to play regularly. I want you guys to write this."

By now my head was spinning. I looked at Moss Klein, my colleague from *The Star-Ledger*, and all we could do was laugh at the absurdity of this entire afternoon. "This is just unbelievable," Klein said. "Now they're even coming into the press box to tell us things."

Pepe's one word of caution to me when I took over the Yankees beat from him was that Steinbrenner was a notorious leaker and that I should be prepared to see stories in the other papers, especially the *Daily News'* chief rival, the *Post*, quoting "sources close to Steinbrenner," saying The Boss was fed up with one player's performance or second-guessing the way the team was being managed. "You have to know the 'source close to Steinbrenner' is always Steinbrenner," Pepe counseled. "That's the way George does things."

I was fortunate in that Steinbrenner was particularly fond of Young—or maybe it would be more accurate to say fearful of him. Young was the most powerful sports columnist in the country, was strongly opinionated, acerbic by nature, and had a glutton for shit-stirring. Nobody wanted to be on the receiving end of Young's vitriol, especially the owner of the Yankees who understood better than most that the best way to tame the beast was to periodically feed him stories.

A couple of days after Christmas in 1984, I was at home in New Jersey when the phone rang. It was Young who, as always, didn't bother to say hello. "Ahhhh, look," he blurted, "the Yankees are signing this guy, Whitson. It's five years, $4.5 million. Just write it."

At the time Ed Whitson was the No. 1 pitcher on the free-agent market. He'd won 14 games for the San Diego Padres in 1984. I knew that his agent, Tom Reich, was a friend of Steinbrenner who had previously steered a few of his clients to the Yankees, so I had a pretty good idea where this was all coming from. "Thanks, Dick," I said. "This is great, but how should I source this?"

"Source? *Source?*" Young screamed. "*I'm* your fucking source!"

My all-time favorite Young [and Steinbrenner] story, which remains one of the most surreal nights of my life, was The Boss' infamous press conference in his hotel suite in the middle of the 1981 Yankees–Dodgers World Series. The Yankees had won the first two games of the series at Yankee Stadium but then lost the next two in Los Angeles, and it began to look as if things were starting to unravel when the Dodgers touched up Guidry for back-to-back solo homers in the seventh inning of Game Five to give them a 2–1 win and a three games-to-two lead in the series. Because the Yankees had an early charter flight back to New York the next morning—in those days the beat writers traveled with the team—I had gone to bed early in my room at the Wilshire Hyatt, where the Yankees were staying, when I was awakened by the ringing of my room phone.

"Billy?" the voice on the line said, "it's Milton. Did I wake you?"

"Well, uh, sort of Milton, what's up?"

"You need to put your pants on, Billy," Milton said. "We're going to a press conference in Steinbrenner's room at 11:30."

As Milton explained it to me, Steinbrenner had gotten into some sort of altercation with a couple of drunken fans earlier in the night and now was summoning all the Yankees writers to his suite for a "briefing." I dressed quickly and joined Milton in the hotel lobby where we then proceeded to take the elevator up to Steinbrenner's suite. I'm not sure if Milton thought I was still working for him or if he merely wanted company.

When we entered the suite, Steinbrenner was standing in the middle of the room with his left hand heavily bandaged, his upper lip puffy, and what looked to be a bump on the right side of his head. He was wearing a bright plaid lumberjack shirt instead of his customary blue blazer and turtleneck. Surrounding him in the room were David Szen, the Yankees' public relations director, the six beat writers from the *Daily News, Post, The New York Times, The Star-Ledger, Newsday,* and *Westchester-Rockland,* and one columnist—Young, who was attired in a purple bathrobe, holding a glass of red wine, and looking somewhat disheveled with his white hair all askew.

As Steinbrenner recounted to the assembled reporters, he'd been on the hotel elevator when two inebriated fans got on. One of them, he said, had a beer bottle in his hand, and the other was wearing a Dodgers hat. Upon recognizing Steinbrenner, they began harassing him, according to Steinbrenner, telling him to "take your choke-ass team back to those animals in New York." He was already in a bad mood, he said, and when the two started to get physical with him, he cold-cocked one of them and threw the other one out of the elevator before getting off himself. "I especially couldn't take them saying my players are chokers," he said. "It's okay for me to criticize them because I pay their checks, but I'm not gonna stand for some drunken fans saying that about them."

At that point, Young got out of his chair and walked across the room to the house phone and began dialing. After a few seconds, he shouted: "This is Young. Get me re-write!"

Steinbrenner, momentarily taken aback, started toward Young, exclaiming: "What are you doing, Dick? This is just a briefing. It's not to be written!"

"The hell it isn't," Young shot back. "A thing like this is news. You don't keep it out of the paper!"

With that Young began dictating a story: "George Steinbrenner comma president of the Yankees comma…" only to be interrupted by Steinbrenner screaming, "I'm not the president of the Yankees, Dick. I'm the *owner* of the Yankees!"

"Oh, yeah," Young slurred, correcting himself and continuing, "was in a fight early this morning with a couple of fans in the hotel where the Dodgers are staying…" only to again be interrupted by Steinbrenner: "The Dodgers? What's wrong with you, Dick? The Yankees! *We're* staying here!"

Suddenly, after imploring Young this was not to be written, Steinbrenner was now serving as his editor as the rest of the writers, whose last deadlines in New York had long since passed, looked on in bemusement. The buffoonery continued the next morning when Steinbrenner boarded the team bus to the airport. With his arm now in a sling, Steinbrenner was greeted by the sound of the theme from *Rocky* from a boom box tape Graig Nettles had somehow found at a nearby record store.

In Steinbrenner's mind he had defended his players' honor, and he no doubt believed his vanquishing of the two ruffians would serve as a rallying point for the team—especially when they landed at Newark Airport and were greeted by the last editions of the *Daily News* on the newsstands with the blaring back page headline: "Steinbrenner KO's 2 in Brawl."

But it was not to be.

Mind you, this was essentially the same Tommy Lasorda-managed Dodgers team the Yankees had defeated in both the 1977 and '78 World Series, and even though they (or at least Steinbrenner) had seemingly lost their grip on this series, I still firmly believed they would find a way to prevail once back home at Yankee Stadium. But Game Six was merely a culmination of all the turmoil surrounding the Yankees throughout the series. The 9–2 trouncing was punctuated by Tommy John waving his arms in disgust and disbelief in the

Yankees dugout in the fourth inning after being pinch hit for by Yankees manager Bob Lemon with the score 1–1.

In the seventh inning, I began typing my column on this ignominious Yankees defeat when I felt a tap on my shoulder from Irv Kaze, the beleaguered Yankees public relations director. "Have you got a minute?" Kaze said. "The Boss wants to see you inside."

I followed Kaze to the back of the press box and through the door to Steinbrenner's dimly lit office, where he was sitting behind his desk flanked by his pal Bill Fugazy, the limousine mogul, and Yankees in-house counsel Ed Broderick. "Quite an embarrassment isn't it, Billy?" George mumbled.

"Well, it's not real good," I replied.

"No, it's not," George said. "It's awful. Humiliating! That's why I called you in here."

Then, shoving a piece of paper across his desk with the official Yankee logo, he said. "I want you to read this over. It's an apology I've written to our fans. I think they deserve this."

I glanced at the paper on which George had inscribed in pen: "I want to sincerely apologize to the people of New York and to the fans of the New York Yankees everywhere for the performance of the Yankee team in the World Series. I also want to extend my congratulations to Peter O'Malley and the Dodger organization—and to my friend Tommy Lasorda, who managed a superb season, playoffs and brilliant World Series." It was signed "George M. Steinbrenner."

"Well, what do you think?"

"I don't know, George," I said. "You're the owner…"

"Yeah, well," Steinbrenner snapped, "I'm gonna have [Yankees venerable public-address announcer] Bob Sheppard read this over the P.A. system after the game."

"I guess if that's what you want to do, George…I just don't know how the players will react."

"I don't give a shit what the players think," he shot back. "They let me down. They let New York down."

As I went back to my seat in the press box, I said to myself, *Steinbrenner is gonna face major backlash over this.* I was just glad he wasn't giving it to me exclusively to print in the *Daily News.* If George's performance in the aftermath of Munson's death had been his finest hour, as Murphy attested, this had been his worst—an impulsive act lambasting his players, who had gotten him to four World Series in six years and won two of them, and made even worse by his effusive praise of Lasorda, the manager they'd beaten two times before. And sure enough, Steinbrenner was roundly criticized in the papers and by his outraged players.

Twenty-seven years later, Gossage told me at his 2008 Hall of Fame induction: "George was the greatest owner I ever played for, but he was crazed that whole 1981 postseason, and after all the shit he pulled in the World Series...the benching of Reggie, the elevator fight, and then the fucking apology, I said to myself: *In two years, I'm out of here.*"

And he was, signing a five-year, $5.5 million contract with the Padres in 1984 that essentially doubled his salary after he refused all overtures from the Yankees. In retrospect I think Goose had a point about that 1981 World Series. In my opinion the Yankees were still the superior team to the Dodgers, and though it can never be quantified, I believe they were subconsciously worn out by Steinbrenner's constant meddling, the firing of managers and general managers every year, and warring with his players. Following the apology it would be another 15 years before the Yankees ever appeared in another World Series.

CHAPTER FIVE

THE GREAT BASEBALL CARD EXPLOSION

In late December of 1985, I got a call from Tom Barnidge, the editor of *The Sporting News,* asking me if I would be interested in being their New York Yankees correspondent. "You'll also be writing a short synopsis piece once a week for us," he said. "We have correspondents for each team in every city, and your friend Moss Klein, who's been doing the Yankees for us these last few years, is moving up to American League columnist."

It didn't matter to me that *The Sporting News* paid the princely sum of $75 for these "letters" (as they termed them), which were essentially just a capsule of the team's news for the week, a rehash of stuff I'd already written for the *Daily News.* Back then, baseball beat writers considered it a privilege to write for *The Sporting News* since it gave them national exposure in a weekly publication with a circulation of more than 500,000. (I suspect the publisher, J.G. Taylor Spink, realized that when nobody ever complained about their rock bottom stipends.)

I'd been reading *The Sporting News*—"The Bible of Baseball" as it was called—since I was 10 years old and was introduced to all the great baseball columnists in the country—Shirley Povich and Bob Addie in Washington, Joe Falls in Detroit, John Steadman in Baltimore, Furman Bisher in Atlanta, Jim Murray and Mel Durslag in Los Angeles, Jerome Holtzman in Chicago, Bob Broeg in St. Louis, Hal Lebovitz in Cleveland, Harold Kaese in Boston, and Earl Lawson in Cincinnati, among others—through it. In my wildest dreams, I never envisioned being one of them.

But about 10 years before Barnidge bestowed the Yankees beat on me, I had come up with an idea, which to my great surprise piqued the interest of Lowell Reidenbaugh, the longtime managing editor of *The Sporting News*. Through the years I'd always been amazed at how little advertising there was in *The Sporting News*. It had just a few small ads in the back of the paper and not for any products but rather baseball card dealers, summer baseball camps, and umpire schools. It was the baseball card dealers' ads that particularly got my attention since I was still a collector myself, and I did business with them. I called Reidenbaugh and, noting that baseball card dealers were among their prime advertisers, pitched the idea of a column devoted strictly to baseball cards. "I like it," Reidenbaugh said. "Let me run it by the people upstairs."

A few days later, Reidenbaugh, who presumably spoke with the people upstairs, meaning the publisher Johnson Spink, J.G. Taylor's son, got back to me and said "start writing." At first it became a biweekly column dealing strictly with baseball cards, but this was around the time the entire sports memorabilia industry was starting to boom, and Reidenbaugh told me I didn't have to restrict myself to just baseball cards.

Then on June 30, 1980, a cataclysmic event happened with baseball cards that wound up having an equally substantial impact on my life. On that date U.S. District Judge Clarence C. Newcomer ruled that Topps, the sole producer of baseball cards since 1956, had "unlawfully restrained and monopolized trade in...pocket-sized pictures of active major league players." The suit had been brought by the Philadelphia-based Fleer Corp, which had been unsuccessful for more than a decade in getting into the baseball card market.

The way Topps had been able to control the baseball card market was to sign all the major league players (and many minor league players as well) to five-year contracts, giving Topps exclusive rights to their photos and facsimile signatures to be sold with confectionary products or alone. The compensation from Topps to the players for these contracts was $5 to sign and $125 a year. That was it. No percentage of sales. Nothing. And for years the players, who didn't know any better, were happy with the $125 just to be part of the Topps baseball card sets.

When Marvin Miller, the newly minted first executive director of the Players Association, was going through the files in his office in 1966 and came across a number of these contracts with Topps, he was aghast. In the years following, he told the player representatives from each team how the players were grossly shortchanging themselves in these contracts with Topps and that their only leverage with Topps was not to sign any future contract renewals.

At the same time, Miller convinced the players on the merits of forming their own joint licensing program in which they would all get a percentage of sales of various licensed products. And although Topps could not come under the licensing program until all those five-year contracts expired, the formation of the licensing wing of the Players Association gave Miller a little leverage to negotiate a substantial improvement in the terms of their contracts with Topps, doubling the payment to $250 annually and giving them 8 percent of the annual sales up to $4 million and 10 percent on sales above that.

In Newcomer's ruling he stated that Fleer would now have the right to seek an agreement with the Players Association to produce their own baseball cards. Suddenly, this was huge news, and as the only person in the country with a column exclusively devoted to baseball cards, I felt I had an obligation to *The Sporting News* to treat this as a news story, not a column, and my first call was to Marvin Miller.

After filling me in on all the history that led up to the lawsuit, Miller could not conceal his elation about Topps losing its monopoly. "So have you granted Fleer a license yet?" I asked.

"They haven't applied to us yet," Miller replied. "But we have already given a license to Donruss."

"Donruss?" I asked. "What's Donruss?"

"They're a small confectionary company, a subsidiary of General Mills based in Memphis," Miller said. "They piggy-backed on the Fleer suit, and when Fleer won, so did they."

Now I had to get the lowdown on this company called Donruss. Miller gave me the name and phone number of Donruss president Stewart Lyman in Memphis. After introducing myself and the nature of my call, I said: "So I guess congratulations are in order here, Mr. Lyman."

He responded with a chuckle. "We're really excited down here," Lyman finally said. "But I have to confess: we know absolutely nothing about baseball."

"That could be a bit of problem," I said, "at least at first anyway."

"You're right. It is," he replied. "We have barely four months to put together a 600-card baseball set in January. We want to be the first set on the market next year. Do you know anyone in baseball who could help us?"

I thought about that for a minute. "As a matter of fact, I might," I said.

"Can you give me some names?" Lyman asked.

"Sure," I said. "Me."

"You?" Lyman said.

"You're gonna need someone directly involved in baseball who can help pick the players for you, write the bios, and compile the stats for the back of the cards," I said. "I can do all of that. To be honest, this would be a dream project for me. I've been collecting baseball cards since 1953 and I've always wanted to be part of the process of creating them."

"This is all good," Lyman said. "I'm gonna fly up to New York next week with some of my people, and we'll meet for dinner to get to know each other and put together a game plan."

On a rainy Friday night in early July 1980, I met with Lyman, vice president of marketing Paul Mullan, and creative design man Neil Lewis at the Milford-Plaza Hotel on Eighth Avenue in Manhattan. After initial introductions and hand-shakes, Lyman ordered a round of drinks, and it was clear to me I was already hired and that he was a man on an urgent mission. "As I told you on the phone, Bill, we have an enormous challenge ahead of us here," Lyman said. "We have to produce a 605-card baseball set in a matter of a few months, something we've never done before at our little confectionary company down in Memphis."

"Well, I don't know anything about the ins and outs of producing the cards," I said, "but I do know what you're going to have to do to make it a set you can all be proud of."

"Give us your thoughts," Mullan said.

"Well," I said, "most importantly, you're gonna need to make your set something that will differentiate it from all the other card companies' sets that will make the kids want to buy your cards over the others."

"So how would you propose we do that?" Lyman asked.

At that moment I suddenly thought about the famous scene in *The Graduate* when Dustin Hoffman's character, Benjamin Braddock, is approached at his graduation party by one of his father's drunken friends who says to him: "I want to say one word to you, just one word: plastics."

"Stewart," I said, "I have only one word for you: rookies."

I then explained to them that in recent years a new rookie card phenomenon had come over the baseball card hobby. It got its genesis in the late '70s. Pete Rose's 1963 Topps rookie card—a card he shared with three other "rookie stars," Pedro Gonzalez of the Yankees, Ken McMullen of the Los Angeles Dodgers, and Al Weis of the Chicago White Sox, and for which there were tens of thousands printed and readily available on the market—was nevertheless being sold on eBay 20 years later for more than $100,000. When I asked around why this could be, it was explained to me that collectors now looked at the first card of potential future Hall of Famers as an investment that would only increase in value through the years, no matter how many of them were produced. "What

I would like to do," I told them, "is flood this first set with rookies. We don't need to have cards of so many backup catchers, .220-hitting utility infielders, and journeymen relief pitchers who kids couldn't care less about. It's the rookies they're gonna want because they've never had cards of them."

Unfortunately, as much as Lyman and his guys liked my great idea about rookies, we were unable to implement it for that first 1981 set. "The reason was," Lewis said, "we didn't have any photographers. We spent weeks scrambling all over the place to get pictures. It was winter. So there were no ballparks to go to shoot photos of players. One of the people who saved us was Keith Olbermann long before he was a big TV star. He was a kid in New York and a baseball card aficionado who'd taken a bunch of pictures of players. He called me up and asked me if I could use any of them. 'Hell yeah,' I told him. But when I asked him how much he wanted for them, he told me, 'Just keep 'em'. He was happy just to have his pictures being made into baseball cards."

In early December Lewis sent me a list of 605 players of whom they were able to obtain pictures. I had printed up form sheets at home with a space for the bios, which I typed in on my trusty Olympia typewriter, and two lines at the bottom for the stats, which I filled in in pencil, and shipped the whole box of them down to Memphis. In retrospect, that first Donruss set in 1981 was an unmitigated disaster.

A good many of the photos were either grainy or out of focus. The cards were printed on flimsy stock, and there were numerous error cards with misidentified players, typos, and wrong stats. Our only consolation was that Fleer's similarly rushed-together first product in '81 was even more fraught with errors and poor quality pictures.

By 1984, however, we had begun to really get our act together, and Lewis' design work clearly outclassed Fleer and Topps. We were now fully emphasizing the use of rookies, though one particular rookie card in that set—Don Mattingly—was not really a rookie. Mattingly came up a little late in 1983 with the Yankees and played in 91 games, but none of the card companies did a card of him. They all did in 1984, but for some reason, the Donruss 1984 Mattingly rookie card is still considered by collectors to be the preeminent card of Donnie Baseball. In '84 and for a few years after, it was selling for as much as $80 in the collectors' market. "The 1984 Mattingly rookie card literally saved Donruss," Lewis said. "We had grossly overproduced our cards the first three years and were losing a lot of money with all the returns. So we decided to significantly downsize our production in 1984, and the result was our most successful set ever largely because the kids all wanted that Mattingly card, and our wax pack sales went through the roof."

A big reason for the rush on Mattingly cards in 1984 was that it was the breakout year for him in which he gave Yankees fans something to be excited about in an otherwise desultory 87–75 season when he and Dave Winfield engaged in a spirited day-to-day battle for the American League batting championship. It made for invigorating daily copy for the Yankees beat writers as well and, as the battle continued into September, it gave me an idea for a baseball card.

I called Lewis down in Memphis and proposed we take advantage of the Mattingly–Winfield batting race, which by this time had captured the attention of the entire nation, with a card entitled "Two for the title" in which we'd have Mattingly and Winfield pose with dueling bats. "That's really cool," Lewis said. "Can you arrange it?"

I assured him I could and when I approached Mattingly with the idea he said: "No problem. Just let me know when you want to do it."

We were on the road in Detroit, and the next morning, I ran into Winfield in the hotel gift shop and pitched the idea to him—only to be stunned when he uncharacteristically started going off on me. "What's in this for you?" he said.

"Nothing," I said. "I don't get a dime more if we do this card or not. I just thought it would be a nice card for the kids to collect next year."

"Well, I don't want to do it," Winfield said with a tone of annoyance in his voice.

"That's your prerogative, Dave," I said. "I don't know why. It would take just a couple of minutes before a game to shoot the picture."

It was then that Winfield revealed a vulnerability that I'd never seen from him and never saw again. "Look," he said, his voice starting to raise, "there's already been too much being made about this batting race, and I don't want to lend any more to it. They're pitting player against player, teammate against teammate, and people are starting to take sides. It's becoming a Black–White thing and it's splitting the clubhouse in half."

Looking back, I can understand now Winfield being upset. From the fans' standpoint, it *had* become a teammate versus teammate thing, and Mattingly was clearly their favorite. Even though Winfield may have felt race also was an issue, it really wasn't. It was more a David (in this case Mattingly) versus Goliath thing. Winfield was the 6'6", 220-pound natural athlete who, upon signing with the Yankees for $23 million, had become the highest-paid player in baseball, while the 6'0", 183-pound Mattingly was the new kid on the block, a self-made, blue-collar player to whom the fans could instantly relate. Even though nobody played the game harder and posted up every day, Winfield, who arrived at the ballpark in his designer suits and a briefcase, could never seem to escape the image of the $23-million man as opposed to Mattingly, whose normal clubhouse attire was blue jeans and a golf shirt.

I decided not to press the issue with Winfield, but we did the card anyway. Instead of a picture of them posing with dueling bats, we had two separate head shots separated by a diagonal "Two for the title" script, which Lewis crafted. At the National Card Convention in 1986, it was voted the 1985 baseball card of the year by *Sports Collectors Digest*. So there was that.

Then in 1986 I doubled down on the rookie cards with a new wrinkle that really set Donruss apart. Using the help of a half-dozen team scouts who concentrated most of their work in the minor leagues, I compiled a list of 20 of the top-rated prospects in baseball on their recommendations and labeled them our "Rated Rookies." That first year of the Rated Rookies, I wanted to make sure I had the crème de la crème of prospects and didn't miss anyone. My scouts agreed the No. 1 prospect in all of baseball was Oakland A's slugger Jose Canseco, who'd torn through Double A and Triple A in 1985, hitting .333 with 27 homers and 127 RBIs in just 118 games before earning a September call-up to Oakland.

When I saw the A's had called Canseco up, I quickly looked at their schedule and was delighted to see they were coming to New York for a weekend series against the Yankees on September 6–8. We were actually past deadline for all the photos for the '86 set, but I implored Lewis to give me an extra day to get a shot of Canseco that first night of the series. New York was one of the few cities where we had a photographer on payroll.

But when I called the photographer and told him what I needed, he said it would be impossible. "We can't shoot at night," he said. "The lighting is terrible."

"I don't give a shit," I said. "We have to have Canseco. You need to go up to Yankee Stadium and figure it out."

As it turned out, not only was it a night game, but it was also raining. Our photographer, however, ingeniously set up a huge spotlight under an umbrella in the visiting dugout and sat Canseco down for a quick head-and-shoulder portrait in his yellow A's warmup jersey. I don't know if I ever felt more gratified about anything in my career than when Canseco went on to become an instant star in the majors, winning American League Rookie of the Year in 1986 and Most Valuable Player in 1988 at the same time his 1986 Donruss Rated Rookie card initially skyrocketed in value to $130 by 1990. Had his career not flamed out through too much steroids, it might still be selling for more than $100, but it remains one of the most iconic baseball cards of the 1980s.

In his Radicards blog, noted baseball card historian Patrick Greenough wrote: "If you were a young collector in the 1980s, you were probably like many other collectors your age and had the 1986 Donruss Jose Canseco Rated Rookie on your most wanted list. At $80–100 this card always seemed far out of reach for most of us. But even as we age, the 1986 Donruss Jose Canseco continues to be a snapshot to a simpler time in collecting, a time when raw cards were king and building sets was still a thing…The colors of his jersey, coupled with those of the card and RR logo along with the image of Canseco with that slight but subtle mustache are just perfect in every way. There isn't a better Rated Rookie Card. It's as if time stood still for just one moment as we're taken back to wishing mom would bring this card home and put it in our stocking to be found on Christmas day."

While compiling the list of 20 Rated Rookies every year, it seemed I was always scrambling to get pictures of one or two of them at the last minute. In some cases it was next to impossible when they were not called up at the end of the season, and we had failed to get a picture of them in the previous spring training. This is what happened with Kevin Morton in 1991. Morton was a soft-tossing, left-handed pitcher who'd had an average year at Double A in 1990. But the scouts all loved him and assured me he was going to be an integral part of the Boston Red Sox rotation at some point in 1991. So he was on my radar all year, and when I was told the Sox were not going to call him up from their

Triple A team in Pawtucket in September, I called our New York photographer Gene Boyars and asked him to take a "road trip" to get a picture of Morton.

As luck would have it, the Triple A Pawtucket Sox were playing in Albany, a short one-hour plane trip from Boyars' home in New Jersey, and I was also able to convince Lewis that we should expense Boyars to purchase a Red Sox cap and Starter warm-up jacket from a local sporting goods store to bring along with him. On the flight up to Albany, Boyars was flipping through the pages of *Baseball America* to see if there were any other potential Rated Rookies on the Pawtucket roster he could shoot while he was there, and there was—Jeff Bagwell.

It would have been nice to have a Rated Rookie card of Bagwell, who was National League Rookie of the Year in 1991 and went on to have a Hall of Fame career, but, alas, it was not to be. "I couldn't believe it," Boyars said. "The day I got there, the Red Sox traded Bagwell to the Astros!"

But at least the Morton quest was a success. Boyars met him at the team hotel, handed him the cap and jacket, took him around to a field behind the building, shot a head-to-shoulders picture of him, and we were the only company to have a card of him in 1991. Unfortunately, Morton did not live up to my scouts' expectations. He made 15 starts for the Red Sox in 1991 with an unimpressive 4.59 ERA and never pitched in the majors again. The last time I looked, his 1991

Rated Rookie card could be had for $1.25 on eBay. Oh well, you can't win 'em all. But the process of creating that card was one of the more delightful experiences for all of us at Donruss.

Much as the Rated Rookies had established Donruss as the go-to company for collectors of rookie cards, another idea I came up with for Lyman after that first misbegotten 1981 set was a 26-card series called "Diamond Kings." Using the hand-painted portraits by renowned baseball artist Dick Perez, it became an instant hit and further set us apart from the other companies. I remarked to Lyman how as a kid I was always enamored by Topps' 1953 baseball card set in which they eschewed the standard photographs of players in favor of artists' paintings. "It's never been done since," I told Lyman, "and I think this would really give us an added touch of class to our set."

I first became acquainted with Perez in 1979 when I saw an ad in *Sports Collectors Digest* for these beautiful, limited edition watercolor postcards of baseball Hall of Famers in the style of the vintage 1880s Allen & Ginter watercolor tobacco cards. They were issued by Perez-Steele Galleries in Fort Washington, Pennsylvania. After purchasing a set of the cards, I thought such a unique new product in the collecting world was worth a column in *The Sporting News*. That led to my introduction to Frank Steele, the CEO of Perez-Steele Galleries. Steele, a longtime aficionado of baseball cards himself, especially the tobacco and caramel issues from the turn of the century, informed me of his close friendship with Perez, who for years had been the official artist and creative design person for the Philadelphia Phillies responsible for all the sketch work in their yearbooks and programs. At one point in our conversation, I mentioned to Steele my longtime appreciation for the 1953 Topps set. "I love that set, too," Steele said.

"Well, I'm thinking about the idea of introducing original artwork to our Donruss set," I said.

"Well, I have just the artist for you," Steele said.

"I know," I said. "Dick Perez does absolutely wonderful work."

From there I introduced Steele to Lyman and Mullan, and a deal was struck to have Perez do 26 paintings—one player for each of the 26 major league teams—and we would make them the first 26 cards in our 1982 set. Collectors loved the Diamond King cards, especially for autograph purposes, and they became a regular staple in all our ensuing Donruss sets.

By the 1990s the baseball card industry had exploded. In 1988 Score became the fourth card company to obtain a license from the Players Association, and the following year, Upper Deck burst onto the scene with a mammoth 800-card baseball set. Not only were there five licensed baseball card companies competing against each other, but all of them were flooding the market with numerous other subsets to their main product. At Donruss we had a 60-card subset of enlarged (3 ½" x 5") cards called "Action All-Stars," an eight-card "Hall of Fame Sluggers" set of Perez paintings, a 56-card "Highlights" set, a 28-card "Super Diamond Kings" set, and a box set of all rookies released in midsummer. The one thing they all had in common was that none of them sold.

Between my day job of covering the Yankees for the *Daily News* and all these additional card sets for which I had to supply copy, I was becoming overwhelmed. In the meantime baseball card shops were cropping up in towns all across the country, and it seemed like almost every newspaper now had a Sunday feature or column in the sports section devoted strictly to baseball cards

In 1983 Donruss was sold by General Mills to Huhtamaki Oy, a food packaging conglomerate in Helsinki, Finland, whose U.S. headquarters was based in Chicago. This led to us in 1985 creating yet another yearly 650-card set called Leaf—slick four-color, double-coated cards on high-quality solid bleach sulfate cardboard to complement our Donruss set. The Leaf set was issued in two series—one in May and the other in midsummer. That enabled us to catch up on all the rookies and traded players we'd missed with the Donruss set. And at least on the Leaf sets, there was room on the back for only one-line bios much to my relief. It was a big hit at first because of the quality of the cards, but collectors soon

Milton Richman, my first mentor at United Press International who taught me so much about being a reporter, and I attend my first World Series in 1975.

I interview Yankees great Mickey Mantle during spring training in 1994. (Neil Waingrow)

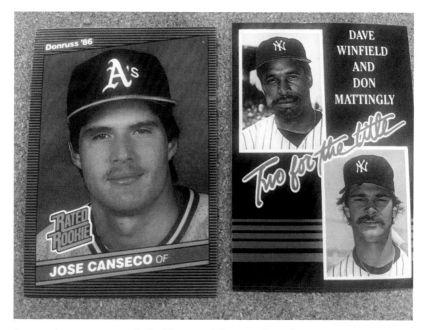

I created two iconic cards for Donruss. The 1986 Jose Canseco "Rated Rookie" card sold for as much as $130 (before he blew up his career with steroids), and the Don Mattingly and Dave Winfield "Two for the title" card was voted 1985 Card of the Year by *Sports Collectors Digest*.

My wife, Lillian, and I hang out with Hall of Fame pitcher Tom Seaver, who became my good friend, at his vineyard atop Diamond Mountain in Calistoga, California, in 2016. I never got enough of his tutorials on winemaking and the art of pitching.

With my friend and co-author, the legendary Don Zimmer, I sign copies of our book, *Zim: A Baseball Life.*

I chat with former Yankees owner George Steinbrenner, who I got to know well but didn't always get along with. (Linda Cataffo / *New York Daily News*)

Sammy Sosa, who had 58 home runs at the time, and slugger Mark McGwire, who had 60 at the time, laugh during a press conference before playing each other on September 7, 1998. We had fun covering the home run chase, but it turns out we were very naive. (AP Images)

On March 17, 2005, Mark McGwire testifies at a hearing on Capitol Hill about the use of steroids in professional baseball while seated next to other stars. My reporting and those of my colleagues helped expose them. (AP Images)

Stan "The Man" Musial entertains everyone Sunday night in the Otesaga lounge with his harmonica riffs of "Orange Blossom Special" and "Wabash Cannonball." That was one of the annual highlights of the Hall of Fame induction ceremonies.

I listen to Ted Williams on the veranda of the Otesaga on the Saturday before the 1999 Hall of Fame induction ceremonies. The "Splendid Splinter" is in the midst of a loud, spirited, and hilarious debate with Tommy Lasorda (not pictured) about who are dumber: pitchers or hitters.

In the spring of 2004, I had a party at Elaine's for my *Pride of October* book. From left to right, Bobby Murcer, Phil Rizzuto, Arlene Howard, Joe Pepitone, and Yogi Berra all came to celebrate with me.

I truly loved legendary manager Sparky Anderson for his brute honesty and outrageous hyperbole. He was a baseball writer's delight, always willing and able to fill our notebooks.

The New York Baseball Writers honor Roland Hemond, one of my dearest friends and an endless fountain of baseball stories, with our most prestigious award: the William Slocum Long and Meritorious Service Award.

On July 24, 1983 at Yankee Stadium, Kansas City Royals third baseman George Brett is restrained by umpire Joe Brinkman and manager Dick Howser as he tries to get to home-plate umpire Tim McClelland. During the famous Pine Tar Game, Brett was ruled out after hitting a two-run home run because his bat exceeded the amount of pine tar allowed. (Getty Images)

While at the Otesaga lounge in Cooperstown, New York, Hall of Famer and former Kansas City Royals third baseman George Brett and I recreate his crazed altercation with umpires at the Pine Tar Game. Much as our little impromptu and inebriated hijinks had provided some funny, last-call theatrics that night in the Otesaga, I then had to inform Brett that he was still out.

realized it, too, was overproduced. Between the overproduction of cards and the proliferation of all the different sets in the market, I found myself getting more and more turned off by all the greed in the baseball card industry. Things were different at Donruss, too. Lyman had left following the sale of the company to Huhtamaki, and Mullan defected to Fleer after he was passed over by the new ownership as CEO.

At the same time, Steele, whom I began to look at as the fox I'd let into the hen house, ingratiated himself to the new CEO and began exercising more and more power behind the scenes, creating all these new subsets, most of which failed miserably. It was Steele, who pushed the company heads to move all the baseball operations from Memphis to Chicago, which meant Lewis, who'd lived in Memphis much of his life, had no choice but to leave. I found Steele meddling on my turf as well, bringing in a young colleague from Philadelphia to select the players for all these new sets.

So in 1989 I quietly left the baseball card business. It had been great fun, riding the crest of the wave, but I was grateful not to have been a part of it when it all came crashing down in the '90s with the disappearance of all the baseball card shops and the demise of Fleer, Score, and ultimately Donruss. Every so often, however, it brings a smile to my face when I open up the drawer of my desk at home and glance at the image of Canseco on his 1986 Rated Rookie card smiling back at me.

CHAPTER SIX

THE CRAZIEST
SEASON OF THEM ALL

The 1981 World Series and all of George Steinbrenner's lunacy culminating in his subsequent apology left the New York scribes in a state of exhaustion. It was generally agreed the New York Yankees had been the better team and were fully capable of making a return trip to the World Series in 1982, but a lot of damage had been done to the team's psyche.

Undaunted, Steinbrenner thought the Yankees just needed to go in a different direction for 1982. The day after the series, he summoned his high command to Yankee Stadium to outline his grand plan. First on the agenda was the free agent status of 35-year-old Reggie Jackson, who in the strike-shortened 1981 season had batted just .237 with a career low 15 homers while battling injuries and periodic verbal barbs from Steinbrenner. In The Boss' view, Jackson was nearing the end of the line—their mutual admiration society was over—and it would be a risk to re-sign him to another long-term contract. And at the organization meeting, he got the reaffirmation he wanted for that from the Yankees' respected hitting coach Charlie Lau, who opined that Jackson's bat had indeed slowed down. "I'm sick and tired of waiting around for the three-run homer," Steinbrenner declared to the group. "The game is changing, and the new emphasis is on speed. That's what I want here: a speed team."

With that, he instructed his chief scout, 69-year-old Birdie Tebbetts, to come up with a list of players with speed who were available either by trade or through free agency. On Tebbetts' recommendation a week after the meeting, the Yankees traded a couple of minor league pitching prospects to the Cincinnati Reds for outfielder Ken Griffey, who'd been an integral part of the Big Red Machine championship teams of the mid-70s. Then two days before Christmas, they outbid the Kansas City Royals and Toronto Blue Jays by a lot—a whopping three-year $2.475 million contract—for Davey Collins, a moderately talented, singles-hitting corner outfielder who would have been much better suited on the artificial turf in Toronto, Kansas City, or Cincinnati, where he'd been the previous four seasons.

Besides jettisoning Jackson, Steinbrenner had planned to not re-sign Lou Piniella and Bobby Murcer, two of his favorites, in order to clear room in the outfield for Griffey and Collins. But then, as he was often wont to do, he hedged his bets and re-signed both of them to "golden parachute" three-year contracts. "I don't know what I'm supposed to do with all these guys," an already beleaguered Yankees manager Bob Lemon said to me on one of the first days of spring training.

Looking over at Collins, he shook his head: "Where am I supposed to play that guy?"

This had been Lemon's second tour of duty as Yankees manager, having led them back from a 14-game deficit in 1978 to their second straight world championship—only to be fired by Steinbrenner the following season, then re-cycled in late August 1981 when The Boss got into a pissing match with Gene Michael. And while once again Lemon was able to guide the Yankees into the World Series, he absorbed the brunt of the blame for the loss to the Los Angeles Dodgers.

In refusing to make a commitment to Lemon for '82, Steinbrenner made frequent off-the-record remarks about his drinking to reporters while simultaneously expressing concerns for his health. But right before the winter meetings in December, Lemon showed up in Tampa, Florida, for a meeting with Steinbrenner, weighing some 24 pounds fewer. As he explained, he had given up hard liquor over the winter and gone on a wine only diet ("it beats quitting," he told the writers later), and the pleasantly surprised Steinbrenner told the media how happy he was to have him back.

Of all the Yankees managers to that point, I'd become especially fond of Lemon, a hard-drinking ex-Navy man and Hall of Fame pitcher with the Cleveland Indians in the '40s and '50s who called everyone "Meat" (which we later learned was a derivative of "Mate"). But poor Lem had no idea of the degree of craziness that had come over Steinbrenner since the 1981 World Series loss when he arrived at Fort Lauderdale, Florida, for spring training. It wasn't long before he was back to hitting the Canadian Club.

The first thing to greet Lemon that spring was the presence of former Olympic Gold Medal hurdler Harrison Dillard wearing a sweatsuit and setting up running drills on one of the back fields. The Cleveland native, Dillard had been an idol of Steinbrenner, who himself had been a champion hurdler at Williams College. "You can't underestimate the importance of speed," Steinbrenner announced to all of us while noting that Dillard would be scrutinizing all the Yankees' running styles and then offering tips on how they could improve their techniques.

While the spectacle of Dillard, stopwatch in hand, conducting daily one-on-one footraces every morning became an unnecessary distraction for Lemon, the writers found it a source of amusement and it made for a steady stream of stories poking fun at the new "streamlined" Yankees—much to the annoyance of Steinbrenner. In particular, the *Daily News*' Mike Lupica began referring to them as the "Bronx Burners," which prompted an enraged Steinbrenner to order Yankees public relations man Irv Kaze to rescind Lupica's spring training credentials. When Kaze explained to Steinbrenner that Lupica's credentials were from the Baseball Writers Association and that he couldn't ban members of the media from spring training, The Boss was not mollified. "Oh yeah?" he shouted to Kaze. "Well, if I see Lupica in camp, then *you're* fired!"

It didn't help either that in the meantime the Yankees played badly throughout the spring, prompting Steinbrenner to hold nightly meetings with Lem and his coaches in his trailer adjacent to the ballpark in which he would relentlessly berate them. One morning I was on the team bus waiting to go to Bradenton, Florida, for a spring training game against the Pittsburgh Pirates when a disconsolate Tebbetts got on and sat down beside me. "This a mess," he said. "We don't know what we're doing here. I would've never recommended we get Griffey and Collins if I knew he was gonna turn around and re-sign Piniella and Murcer."

In Piniella's case Steinbrenner had also inserted a weight clause in the contract, requiring him to come into camp under 200 pounds. This became a major source of contention and triggered a whole other spring training comedy show for the writers. Over the winter Steinbrenner had assigned Howard "Hopalong" Cassidy, the former Ohio State Heisman Trophy winner who was working for the Yankees as a minor league coach and special fitness instructor, to conduct daily workouts with Piniella at a local high school track in Tampa. But as Piniella told me with much bemusement years later, he turned the tables on Steinbrenner by instead talking "Hoppy" into doing the workouts while he sat in the stands with a cup of coffee, a stopwatch, and a newspaper.

Consequently, Piniella reported to Fort Lauderdale a not-so-svelte 210 pounds, whereupon Steinbrenner announced he would be fining him $1,000 a day until he got down to 200. This began spirited war of words between Steinbrenner and Piniella that lasted for a week and dominated the back pages of the New York tabloids. All I could think of was Buddy Martin's famous words when he hired me to be the *Daily News* Yankees beat writer: "Steinbrenner thinks he owns the back page of this newspaper, and you know what? He probably does."

At one point Piniella called the beat writers together at West Palm Beach, Florida, before a game against the Montreal Expos, pacing up and down and venting: "I am utterly disgusted by George Steinbrenner and his policies. I'm being treated like a 19-year-old and I find that insulting. I'm not happy with these damn fines. I'm like Smith-Barney. I've worked hard for my money, and he's treating me like Little Orphan Annie."

To that, Steinbrenner responded: "Sometimes Lou needs to be treated like a 19-year-old. I've got the weight requirement right here in black and white. He knew what he was signing. If my employer was paying me $350,000, which is more than the president of the United States is making, I'd sure as hell take seven pounds off and honor that contract!"

Meanwhile, in an effort to "help" Lou lose the weight, Steinbrenner instructed Lemon to play him in afternoon B games before the A games at night with no off days. Matters reached a breaking point after one night game when the Yankees were running wind sprints in the outfield, which Steinbrenner ordered after losses, and Piniella casually tossed a stray baseball into the stands, and then Lemon told him to retrieve it. There were hardly any fans left in the stadium, and the writers had also long since finished writing their stories and departed. So the angry scene that ensued—Piniella charging after Lemon like a raging bull and the two nearly coming to blows—would probably have never been reported had it not been for Liz Harper, the wife of John Harper, who was then a fledgling reporter for the *Morristown Record*, a small paper in New Jersey, and later my *Daily News* colleague.

Moss Klein, the beat reporter for *The Star-Ledger*, and I were having drinks at a favorite watering hole a few blocks from Fort Lauderdale Stadium when we ran into Liz, who said she was waiting there for her husband who was still finishing up his story at the ballpark. "That was quite a fight afterward, huh?" she said.

"Excuse me," I said, "What fight?"

"Oh," Liz said. "You guys didn't see it? After the game Piniella and Lemon went at it in the outfield. It was right in front of me. I heard Piniella screaming about having to pick up a ball and then going after Lemon. It was quite something."

Moss and I looked at each other, stunned, then instinctively took out our notebooks and scribbled down the details of Liz's account. We then made a beeline for the men's room where there was a pay phone. But this was one time I lost a footrace, and as Moss grabbed the phone, I frantically looked around and dashed into the ladies' room where the only other phone in the place was located. Fortunately, it was late, and there were no women in there as I dictated my Lemon–Piniella fight story to the office. A few minutes later we both emerged from the respective restrooms, looked at each other, and laughed. "This is really a first," I said to Moss. "I have just dictated a story to my office of a fight I didn't see from the ladies' room of a bar!"

Meanwhile, as the Yankees continued hurtling to their eventual disheartening 9–16 spring training record, Steinbrenner became more and more panicked and by mid-March had decided to abandon the speed game plan and attempted to turn the power back on with a few ill-conceived trades that only further glutted up the roster. On March 24 the Yankees acquired Butch Hobson, an oft-injured right-handed hitting first baseman/designated hitter from the Angels who failed to hit a single homer for the Yankees, batting .172 before being released after just 30 games.

Then, in an even more head-scratching trade, the day before the season opened, Steinbrenner sent Ron Davis, the promising, young hard-throwing reliever, and top shortstop prospect Greg Gagne to the Minnesota Twins for shortstop Roy Smalley. Though a decent hitter who'd been in an All-Star in 1979 with 24 homers, Smalley had limited range at short, and his $600,000 contract had become too expensive for the Twins. Steinbrenner made the trade on the advice of his friend Sid Hartman, the columnist for *The Minneapolis Star*, even though the very popular and defensively steady Bucky Dent was still the Yankees shortstop. Later that year, Gene Michael told me ruefully: "That was one of the worst trades we ever made. It weakened two of our biggest strengths: the bullpen and our infield defense. But George was always listening to outside people like Sid Hartman rather than his own."

One of the few bright spots in the spring of '82 had been the emergence of left-hander Dave Revering, who surprised everyone by hitting over .400 and—temporarily—winning the first-base job. The 29-year-old Revering, a soft-spoken, laid-back Californian, was a pleasant enough fellow but always seemed to be in another world, blithely detached from the daily Yankees circus. Unfortunately, on the last weekend of spring training, he hurt his knee tripping on a seam on the artificial turf in the New Orleans Superdome and never regained his hitting stroke. At the end of April, Revering was hitting .150 with no homers and was abruptly traded to the Blue Jays for 33-year-old John Mayberry, a one-time prodigious lefthanded slugger who was now past his prime but still in the middle of a four-year, $3.2 million contract, which the Blue Jays were more than happy to unload on Steinbrenner.

The day of the Revering–Mayberry trade, May 5, was supposed to be a travel day to Seattle for the Yankees, but because New York lost a 9–7 game in extra innings to the Oakland A's the night before, Steinbrenner ordered what Goose Gossage bitterly termed a "punishment workout" at Yankee Stadium before the team departed for Seattle. Fortunately for the writers, the weary Yankees players had plenty of scathing quotes about Steinbrenner to take care of our off-day stories, but then shortly before we were to get on the team bus to the airport, Kaze called us aside to inform us of the trade. "I'm giving you guys this now," he said, "so you can call it into your offices when we get to Seattle. We're not announcing it yet."

By that, Kaze meant the Yankees weren't announcing the trade to anyone, including Revering, who much to our surprise was seen boarding the plane with all the other players. When we arrived at our hotel in Seattle and got on line for our room keys, the bewildered Revering was presented with a plane ticket back across the country to Toronto.

An addendum to the Revering saga was a conversation I had with then-Blue Jays manager Bobby Cox the following spring that elicited one of the most colorful quotes I ever got from anyone in all my years as a baseball writer. Over the winter the Blue Jays had acquired Cliff Johnson, a notorious clubhouse disrupter, to replace Revering and Wayne Nordhagen, who'd hit one homer for them in '82 with just 20 RBIs in 197 plate appearances, as their designated hitter. I mentioned to Cox that Johnson was hardly his kind of player. "Why would you ever want this guy on your team?" I asked.

"Did you see who I had for my DHs last year?" Cox replied. "One guy was fuckin' finished, and the other guy was fuckin' nuts."

An even more misguided trade on Steinbrenner's part in the spring of '82 was the one he ordered for Doyle Alexander, a perpetually disgruntled right-handed starting pitcher who was embroiled in a nasty contract dispute with the San Francisco Giants and had sat out the entire spring. The trade for Alexander was able to be consummated only after Steinbrenner agreed to sign him to a new four-year, $2.2 million contract. The day before the trade was announced, I was tipped off to it by acting Yankees general manager Bill Bergesch, who was not at all happy about having to give up a couple of top Yankees prospects for him.

But before I wrote my story, I needed to call Lemon, who I knew was in his room at the Yankees spring training hotel, the Galt Ocean Mile, watching his favorite TV show, *Barnaby Jones*. "I hear you've got a new pitcher, Lem," I said.

"Oh yeah?" he said. "Who am I getting? I'm always the last one to know around here."

"Doyle Alexander," I announced.

After a long pause and a sigh, Lem replied: "Just what I need: another hemorrhoid."

There couldn't have been a more appropriate description. For that's what Alexander was for the next year and a half with the Yankees, though, at least for his sake, Lemon was spared having anything to do with him. When spring training ended, it had become painfully obvious that Tebbetts' assessment of the team to me was right. The '82 Yankees were a total mess, and though Lemon had been promised a full year by Steinbrenner, he was already worn out by mid-April.

The first road trip of the season was to Texas, Detroit, and Chicago. The team was off our first night in Chicago, and Lem announced he wanted to take the writers and the coaches to Miller's Pub for cocktails and ribs. On the way from the hotel to Miller's, I wound up sharing a taxi with Lemon, who'd been delayed by another haranguing phone call from Steinbrenner. "I've had it, Meat," Lem suddenly said.

"What do you, mean, Lem? I asked.

"I can't take this anymore. I've had it with this guy. No matter what I do, I can't please him. I'm going to quit."

"You can't be serious?" I said.

"As serious as I've ever been. I don't need this aggravation. Life is too short. I'm only telling you this because you've been a good friend. I just can't take it anymore."

As I pondered what he was telling me, I abandoned my role as a reporter and tried to reason with him. "Don't quit, Lem," I said.

"Why?"

"Because if you do, you're liable not to get your money. If nothing else, all the aggravation he's put you through has to be worth something, and I'd hate for that to happen to you. Play it out. Let him fire you, but don't quit."

We sat silent for a minute.

"Okay, I'll think about it," Lem finally said. "But right now I want to have some drinks with my friends."

When we arrived at Miller's, I thought of what had just transpired in the back of the taxi cab. I had just talked the manager of the New York Yankees out of quitting, but this would've been one scoop I wanted no part of. It would've been a betrayal of Lem's confidence, and I knew if he saw it splashed all over the back page of the *Daily News* he would've regretted it the next day.

After the Yankees won both games against the White Sox in Chicago, they came home and lost three of four to the Tigers at Yankee Stadium, leaving them 6–8 on April 25th. The next day, an off day for the Yankees, Steinbrenner fired Lemon and replaced him as manager with Gene "The Stick" Michael. Lemon was out of his misery, but at least he got his money, and I wasn't sure who was more relieved: Lem or me.

As it had been for Lemon, this was also the second time around as Steinbrenner's manager for Stick, who the year before agreed to step down as Yankees GM to replace Dick Howser as the manager. He then clashed daily with The Boss before being fired September 5 with about a month left in the regular season. As per his nature, Steinbrenner immediately felt remorse at firing Michael, whom he said he regarded as a "son."

To which Michael retorted: "Then why did you fire me?"

"Oh c'mon, Stick," Steinbrenner said. "Why would you have wanted to stay manager and be second-guessed by me every day when you can come upstairs and sit with me and be one of the second-guessers?"

It was actually good advice, but once Steinbrenner decided that the 61-year-old Lemon just wasn't up to the job in '82, he had nowhere to turn for a new manager. Billy Martin, his usual go-to guy, was now managing the A's, and Stick was right there, serving as his top Yankees advisor. But it took just one game for Stick to realize the second time around with Steinbrenner was going to be no different than the first. Maybe even worse.

For his "second" debut just happened to be the same night Jackson made his first visit back to Yankee Stadium as a member of the Angels with whom he'd signed as free agent over the winter. Ron Guidry was pitching for the Yankees, who trailed 2–1 when Jackson came to bat to lead off the seventh. He proceeded to hit a titanic home run off the right-field, upper deck façade. As Jackson triumphantly toured the bases, the Yankee Stadium crowd of 35,458 looked to the owner's box and erupted spontaneously in chants of "Steinbrenner sucks!"

After the game, which was cut short by a tremendous rainstorm, an apoplectic Steinbrenner summoned Stick and his coaches up to his office. As Stick later related to me: "We got up there, and George is standing by his desk, and as I walked in the room, he says to me: 'You're killing me, Stick! Can you believe that? My first game and this fucking guy says, I'm killing him!'"

I later learned that overnight Steinbrenner had ordered his security chief Pat Kelly to go down to the visiting clubhouse and perform a (blatantly illegal) X-ray examination of Jackson's bats, and they indeed found one that was loaded. When years later I asked Kelly what they had done with the bat and why nothing was ever said by Steinbrenner—or even Jackson—about it, he said they sawed it up in pieces and threw it in the garbage. After all, they couldn't very well have sent it to the commissioner's office.

Meanwhile, it didn't take long for Stick to realize how much of a "hemorrhoid" he had inherited in Alexander. Having missed most of spring training because of his contract holdout, Alexander didn't make his first Yankees start until April 24, when the Tigers bombed him for three homers and five earned runs in six innings. Two weeks later on May 6, his season was abruptly interrupted—by his doing—when he was removed by Michael after three innings. The victim of four unearned runs, Alexander took out his frustrations by punching a dugout wall and fractured a knuckle on his pitching hand in the process. "It was a dumb thing to do, one of the dumbest things I've ever seen," Michael said. "He was important to our plans and he's not only hurt himself. He's hurt the team."

Alexander did not return to action until July 8, having been fined $12,500 by the Yankees for his stupidity, but that start was even more of a disaster. The Yankees had sent him to their Triple A farm team in Columbus, Ohio, to pitch himself back in shape, but when Steinbrenner requested he stay a little longer there, he refused. Infuriated, Steinbrenner ordered Michael to activate him immediately and pitch him against the A's in Oakland, which resulted in him being pounded for five runs in just an inning and a third. After the game Bergesch issued a statement to the media, obviously dictated by Steinbrenner, that said: "What Alexander did tonight was disgraceful but typical of the selfishness of the modern-day players."

Alexander continued to struggle in his next five starts until hitting his nadir in Detroit, on August 10, when the Tigers bombarded him for three homers and six runs in three innings, prompting another even more outrageous statement from Steinbrenner—and a lot of amusing reactions from the Yankees players to fill our notebooks. This time Steinbrenner allowed Bergesch to use his name in declaring: "After what happened tonight, I'm having Doyle Alexander flown back to New York to undergo a physical. I'm afraid some of our players might get hurt playing behind him. He steadfastly refused to go back to Columbus another time to pitch his way back into shape. That's okay if you back it up with performance, but Alexander has given up eight homers in 38 innings and in his last two starts 11 runs in five innings. Obviously, something is wrong, and we intend to find out."

In the clubhouse afterward, the Yankees players treated this latest Steinbrenner salvo with both anger and amusement. "Doyle may be getting a physical," Gossage said, "but George needs a mental."

Asked if he feared playing behind Alexander, Graig Nettles cracked: "I wasn't worried. Maybe I might have if I was sitting in the left-field stands."

For his part Alexander conceded that maybe going back to New York for a physical was a good move but added: "I want to make it plain this is with a medical doctor, not a psychiatrist. A lot of people are going crazy around here, but I'm not one of them."

It never got any better for Alexander, and he finished the 1982 season 1–7 with a 6.08 ERA for the $500,000 Steinbrenner was paying him. The following March, he surprised the writers by pitching three shutout innings against the Baltimore Orioles in his first spring training start. But when I ran down to the clubhouse to interview him about this potential new beginning for him, I was greeted by silence. "You're probably wondering why I'm not answering any of your questions," he finally said to me.

"Well, yeah," I said.

"The reason is I haven't forgotten all the things you wrote about me last year," he said. "As far as I'm concerned, I have nothing to say to you."

"Okay, Doyle, if that's how you feel," I said. "I only wrote what I saw. You had a lousy season. I think even you would have to admit that. I didn't rip you unfairly."

"It doesn't matter," he said. "You continue writing. I'll continue pitching. Your job is to observe me and write it. I'm not going to help you by giving you quotes. You just observe."

And that's the way it ended between me and Dour Doyle. I continued to observe him for eight more winless appearances with the Yankees in 1983 before Steinbrenner released him on May 31 with $1.5 million remaining on his contract.

For the Stick it all came to a crashing end in '82 on August 3 after just 86 games, when the Yankees suffered a doubleheader loss to the White Sox. After the second game, in which they were drubbed 14–2, Steinbrenner ordered Bob Sheppard to read a statement over the public-address system, informing all the fans in attendance they would be entitled to free tickets to any future Yankees games that season. "When I heard that," Michael said, "I knew I was gone again."

Later that night, as the writers were finishing up their game stories, Steinbrenner marched into the press room and announced he was firing Michael and replacing him with his senior advisor and periodic pitching coach Clyde King and adding: "I will take no questions."

At the time of Stick's firing, the Yankees were 50–50, in fifth place, and eight-and-a-half games behind. They were 29–33 the rest of the way under King to finish with their first losing record since 1969. The tumultuous 1982 Yankee season, in which Steinbrenner ran through three managers, five pitching coaches, three batting coaches, and a then-record 47 players, had mercifully come to an end.

CHAPTER SEVEN

LEGENDS
AND CROOKS

I'd been writing my innocent baseball cards/collecting column for *The Sporting News* for a few months when I got a call from Barry Halper, a wealthy New Jersey businessman and CEO of a large paper products company who claimed to have the greatest collection of baseball memorabilia ever assembled, including that of the Hall of Fame in Cooperstown. "You've got to come to my house and see this," Halper said. "I guarantee you're gonna want to write about my collection. There's nothing like it anywhere."

Halper kept pestering me until finally in July 1976 I made the trek to his spacious 4,500-square foot home in Livingston, New Jersey, in which the entire lower level was devoted to wall-to-wall baseball artifacts, thousands of signed baseballs, hundreds of bats and signed gloves, autographed 19th century photographs and letters, contracts, posters, statues, and the largest collection of uniforms anywhere, all of which were arranged on a computerized revolving dry cleaner's carousel. I spent the entire day there, leaving with the realization that I'd seen only the tip of the iceberg. As Halper escorted me out the front door, he instructed me to look up to the roof of his house at what appeared to be a very primitively constructed weather vane of two old bats. "It was Roger Connor's," Halper said proudly in reference to the 19th century Hall of Fame New York Giants home run champion. "I saw an old picture of it in my friend Marty Appel's book, *Baseball's Best*, on top of what was said to be Connor's old house in Waterbury, Connecticut. I knew I had to have it if I could find it. So I called the census bureau in Waterbury and asked for the address of the old Connor home only to find out it had been turned into a masonry. I called the masonry, introduced myself to the guy in charge there, and told him I wanted to buy the weather vane on top of his building. I'm sure the guy thought I was nuts, but when I told him what I was willing to pay for it, he arranged to have one of his people go up on the roof and take it down and hand it over to me. Later when I got home and installed it on top of my own house, I sent him a week's supply of toilet paper from my company in appreciation, which must have really blown his mind."

I knew right then there was a whole lot more to Halper's vast baseball collection than just the artifacts themselves. Rather, it was the stories behind the *pursuit* of those artifacts, the lengths to which Halper would go in his quests to obtain them—all of which made him one of the most amusingly obsessed people I ever met. In the months and years to come, I made many more visits to the Halper home, never tiring of his tales of collecting triumphs, and we became fast friends to the day he died at age 66 in November of 2005.

Above all, Halper was obsessed with Babe Ruth, to whom he believed he actually had a spiritual connection in that his wife Sharon's father's name was George, and George had a brother named Herman and a sister named Ruth, completing the Babe's full given name. Halper even looked a little like the Babe, and some of his most cherished artifacts were the famous polo coat Ruth is seen wearing in his last appearance at Yankee Stadium in 1948 and the actual sequence of letters between Boston Red Sox owner Harry Frazee and New York Yankees owner Jacob Ruppert for Ruth's bill of sale to the Yankees in 1919.

He got the polo coat from a reverend in North Conway, Massachusetts, who'd seen Halper on NBC's *Today* show and had been given it by Ruth's daughter in the 1950s and kept it in a closet all those years. The bill of sale letters fell into Halper's lap when a guy in Riverdale, New York, who lived in a house once owned by Ruppert, called him and offered them to him for free after finding them among a box of other papers in a closet he was cleaning out.

Halper loved the chase as much as the actual acquisitions. We were together in Chicago in July 1983 for the 50th anniversary of All-Star Game, which was a collecting smorgasbord for Halper because Major League Baseball invited all the living players from the original 1933 All-Star Game at Comiskey Park. He brought with him a trunk full of old uniforms, bats, caps, gloves, and photos to get signed. On the night before the game, there was a banquet for the All-Stars—past and present—at the headquarters hotel, and I spotted Halper sitting in the lobby with a bat and a musty old Cleveland Indians cap, which he informed me had been those of Earl Averill, the Hall of Fame Indians outfielder in the '30s who famously had hailed from Snohomish, Washington. Spying this withered old man waiting for the elevator, Halper jumped up and exclaimed, "There he is!" He dashed across the lobby with the bat, cap, and an old program. "Earl!" he shouted. "The Earl of Snohomish! I need you to sign these!"

Earl, who was accompanied by his wife, looked at Halper, bewildered. "Maybe in the morning," said his wife.

"No, no," Halper said, "we can do it now. It'll take just a minute. I'll come up to the room with you!"

And with that the three of them disappeared into the elevator. About 10 minutes later, Halper re-appeared out of the elevator—holding aloft the bat, cap, and photo all signed by the "Earl of Snohomish"—with a huge grin of satisfaction on his face.

"Barry," I said, "you're crazy."

"I know," he said. "I just have to."

But that wasn't the end of the story. The next day Halper called me in my hotel room, sounding very excited. "You're not gonna believe what just happened here," he said. "They just carried someone out the front door on a stretcher into an ambulance, and wouldn't you know it was Earl Averill!" It seemed the 81-year-old Averill had suffered a stroke, from which he never recovered and died a couple of weeks later. Haper loved telling that story how it was his opportunistic good fortune to get the very last Averill autographs.

Another time I was sitting in George Steinbrenner's private box as Halper's guest at the old Yankee Stadium on a day Richard Nixon, a huge baseball fan, happened to be right behind us. Halper always had a few baseballs at the ready for just such an occasion and he asked the former president if he would mind signing them. Nixon happily agreed, but as he began to sign the balls, I winced when Halper asked: "Would you mind signing one of them 'Tricky Dick'?"

I was sure one of Steinbrenner's security people was going to throw us out of the box right there, but Nixon was remarkably unruffled. "Oh, I can't do that, Barry," he said, "but how about just 'the Trickster'?"

"You're the only person I know who could get away with this shit," I said to Halper later. "Anybody else would get thrown out of the box. But they all look at you as this sweet, innocent fan."

It seemed every week Halper would call me with more tales of exciting new acquisitions, especially uniforms. He had more than a thousand of them on that dry cleaning carousel, including multiple Ruths and Lou Gehrigs, and it was his mission to have at least one uniform from every Hall of Famer. He was well on his way to that goal when one day he was contacted by Ollie O'Mara, an old shortstop with the Brooklyn Dodgers from 1914 to 1918 who claimed to have in his possession a number of uniforms from the old Baltimore Orioles, who won three consecutive National League pennants from 1894 to 1896 before merging with the Brooklyn Dodgers.

O'Mara himself had quite a colorful history. After his playing days, he and his brother, John, were notorious bookmakers in their hometown of Kenosha, Wisconsin, and after being indicted for bribery, bookmaking, and operating an illegal race track wire, Ollie went on the lam for 15 years until the federal case against him was eventually abandoned. He was living in Reno, Nevada, when he got in touch with Halper. "He told me he had all these uniforms, which he'd gotten from Wilbert Robinson, who was his manager with the Dodgers," Halper told me. "This was a mother-lode of impossible-to-find 19th century Hall of Famers: Dan Brouthers, Wilbert Robinson, Wee Willie Keeler, Joe Kelley, and Hughie Jennings."

The only catch was O'Mara would only sell them to Halper one at a time or whenever he said, "he needed gambling money."

Halper bought the Brouthers uniform jersey first and then waited anxiously every few months until O'Mara called him looking for more "stake." It took more than a year, but he eventually got all five, and then O'Mara called him and said he had another Hall of Famer's uniform from Zack Wheat, his former teammate who played for the Dodgers from 1909 to 1926. This got me to thinking. "Don't you think it's rather curious that the only uniforms O'Mara has are of Hall of Famers?" I asked Halper. "How did he know back then they were gonna be Hall of Famers?"

"He probably has more," he replied, "but figures I'm only going to pay top dollar for the Hall of Famers."

In amassing his incredible collection, Halper was both ingenious and tireless. He spent countless hours combing through Legacy.com and Ancestry.com to track down the relatives of old players and was an active bidder on all the auction houses advertising in *Sports Collectors Digest*. His extensive collection of Gehrig memorabilia—uniforms, contracts, photos, etc.—he got mostly from Gehrig's widow, Eleanor, who was a regular guest at Yankee Stadium for Opening Day and Old-Timers' Day.

Once a month he'd pay a visit to Eleanor at her apartment on East 53rd Street, and they'd talk about her husband, Ruth, and all the old Yankees of the '20s and '30s, and he'd invariably leave with another valuable Gehrig memento for his collection. For her part Eleanor welcomed her visits from Halper. She loved reminiscing about the old days, loved the attention from a limited Yankees partner, and especially loved the case of her favorite scotch Halper always brought with him.

One day in the spring of 1994, I got a call from Halper sounding uncharacteristically distressed. "There's something funny going on with these auction houses that advertise in *SCD*," he said. "You see these uniforms selling for record prices, uniforms that I bid on and didn't get, and then a month later, the same uniforms show up in a different auction house. I need you to look into this!"

I followed the same auctions in *Sports Collector's Digest* that Halper did but didn't really think much of the frequent record prices being paid for old uniforms—such as the $363,000 paid for a 1927 Gehrig road Yankees jersey in a San Francisco-based Richard Wolffers auction in October 1992—other than an enlightenment as to how the baseball memorabilia business, particularly the old uniforms, had really exploded in the '90s. My main collecting interest then was in baseball cards where I'd become acquainted with Alan

"Mr. Mint" Rosen, the legendary self-proclaimed "Million Dollar Baseball Card Dealer," who would travel anywhere with a suitcase full of cold hard cash to purchase collections of old cards. "Mr. Mint" also dabbled in the auction business and was intimately familiar with all the players in it, honest and otherwise. When I mentioned Halper's concerns to him and his solicitation of me to look into it, he laughed. "You're not gonna want to go there, Madden," he said. "It's an out-of-control hobby full of crooks."

Nevertheless I did go there with the help of Halper and "Mr. Mint." And after months of investigation with one dealer after another lying to me, the *Daily News* was able to produce a two-part, page one series titled "Collector Curveball," which ran May 29–30, 1994 and exposed an industry rife with deception, shill bidding, secret deals, and outright fraud. I first focused on the Wolffers Auction House in San Francisco, whose president, Duane Garrett, was a popular talk show host on KGO-AM radio in San Francisco and a big-time Democratic Party fundraiser with close ties to then-vice president Al Gore and California senator Diane Feinstein, because that was the house Halper particularly had cited as manipulating all those seemingly phony uniform deals.

In November of 1991, Wolffers offered a 1957 Brooks Robinson Orioles "rookie" jersey for $10,000 to $12,500, which, as soon as it was pictured in their catalogue, was deemed a fake by Phil Wood, a local Baltimore radio broadcaster and an acknowledged expert on Orioles memorabilia. "There were so many things wrong with that jersey, starting with the fact that it was Rawlings jersey when Spalding was the company that manufactured Orioles jerseys in 1957," Wood told me. Despite Wood's public condemnation of the jersey, Garrett sold it anyway.

That same year a 1941 Hank Greenberg Detroit Tigers home uniform, which numerous knowledgeable collectors insisted was also a fake, was sold by Wolffers for $85,000. Ed Rudnick, a respected Detroit-based dealer and collector, told me he wrote a letter to Garrett citing a number of issues with the Greenberg jersey that deemed it bogus. "I included a photo of Greenberg in 1941 in his Tiger uniform with a block letter No. 5 on the back as opposed to a rounded No. 5 on the jersey Garrett was trying to sell," Rudnick said. "He never got back to me."

Three years later it was reported that same 1941 Greenberg jersey had been sold for a grossly discounted $22,000 by Sports Heroes, a publicly traded sports memorabilia company in my hometown of Oradell, New Jersey. Upon further investigation I was able to discover that Sports Heroes had also sold the bogus 1957 Robinson jersey. It seemed Sports Heroes, which did a lot of back-and-forth deals with Wolffers, had been paying inflated prices for numerous uniforms, bats, and gloves and wound up trading or selling them at a loss. Not long after our *Daily News* exposé, it went out of business.

Meanwhile, another Wolffers-auctioned uniform that caused much consternation—that 1927 Gehrig road jersey, which I later discovered had also been consigned by Sports Heroes before reportedly being sold for $363,000—actually had sold for far less. I was able to learn the winning bidder only put up $74,000, and Garrett threw in a Ty Cobb uniform to which he affixed a grossly inflated $300,000 credit. Until then, the highest price a Cobb uniform had ever netted in the collectors' market was $176,000. When I contacted Garrett in San Francisco, he said he didn't exactly remember what the trade was, adding, "I only know the Cobb was a beautiful uniform."

"Right," I said. "I'm sure it was."

As it turned out, selling bogus memorabilia and manipulating auction prices was the least of Garrett's deceit. On July 26, 1996, he jumped to his death off the north tower of the Golden Gate Bridge, and it was later discovered in court papers that he'd run up more than $11 million in debts.

The more I began digging into the Wolffers' scandal, the more I came to realize what a quagmire of unending fraud and corruption the entire sports memorabilia auction business was. "Mr. Mint" had been right. It *was* an out-of-control hobby full of crooks, especially when it came to uniforms.

Another shady memorabilia company that kept coming up was Grey Flannel Collectibles, whose proprietors, Richard Russek and Andy Imperato, were involved in a number of suspect transactions, not the least of which was their "authenticating" the blatantly fake 1941 Greenberg Tigers jersey. At the National Sports Collectors Convention in Atlanta in July 1992, Russek and Imperato were squarely in the middle of another shady transaction involving a grease-stained 1942 Red Sox uniform that purportedly had been worn by Hall of Famer Jimmie Foxx.

The Foxx uniform was being auctioned at the National by Superior Galleries of Beverly Hills, California, who in turn had enlisted Imperato to authenticate it. Word had spread through the National that a wealthy collector from Connecticut named Howard Rosenkrantz, who reportedly had uniforms of every member of the 500 homer club except Foxx, had let it be known he had to have it "at whatever cost" and commissioned Russek to do his bidding for him.

According to several witnesses, the bids on the Foxx uniform kept getting higher and higher, but when it got into six figures, the only bidder anyone saw in the room was Russek, whose bid of $200,000 won the day and left veteran dealers and savvy collectors flabbergasted. "For one thing the uniform looked like it was run over by a truck," said noted dealer and consultant for Sotheby's, Bill Mastro. "I can't prove it, but I have my doubts [that] legitimate bidding was going on. There was no way that uniform could go for that figure."

When I contacted Rosenkrantz, he admitted he didn't feel good about the way the auction had gone down. "Russek told me he didn't see anyone else bidding against him," Rosenkrantz said. "In retrospect I guess that sounds kind of flimsy...To be honest I thought the highest I would have to go was $150,000." As for Russek's partner Imperato also authenticating the uniform, Rosenkrantz said: "Andy's my friend, but I have a bad taste about this thing."

A similar tale of Grey Flannel's dubious role as both authenticators and brokers, in what I had come to conclude was a totally unregulated baseball auction business, involved a much-traveled 1937 Gehrig road jersey. Imperato claimed he'd obtained the jersey from a sportswriter in the Midwest, wrote a letter of authenticity on it, and arranged its sale to a wealthy ophthalmologist in southern New Jersey, who then reportedly traded it through Imperato to—guess who?—Sports Heroes. The uniform was then put in a Christie's auction, received no bids, and then Sports Heroes—again through Imperato— traded it to Halper.

"Andy Imperato is like one of those Wild, Wild West sheriffs," Rosen said to me, laughing. "He's both judge and jury. All his uniforms are good, and nobody hangs in his courtroom as long as he gets a piece of the deal."

By this time, I was disgusted with all these people and disappointed to realize my friend Halper, who got me involved in investigating them all in the first place, was a party—however unwittingly—to a lot of these uniform shenanigans. I knew a lot of his uniforms he'd obtained one way or another through Grey Flannels and I wondered how many of them were bad. "I don't understand why you're getting in bed with these con artists," I told him. "They're all crooks and can't be trusted."

Even Mastro, the kingpin of dealers of that time, turned out to be the biggest crook of them all. He was exposed by Teri Thompson and Michael O'Keeffe, my colleagues at the *Daily News*. Thompson had been an award-winning sportswriter and columnist at the *Rocky Mountain News* and ESPN when she was hired by the *Daily News* in 2000 to establish a sports investigative unit. One of the primary investigative series she and O'Keeffe produced for the *Daily News* (and which also was turned into a much-acclaimed book, *The Card*) was the long and twisted tale of the famous T-206 Honus Wagner cigarette card that in 2007 was sold by Mastro for $2.8 million to Arizona Diamondbacks general partner Ken Kendrick.

The T-206 Wagner card had long been considered the crown jewel of baseball cards with only 20 to 25 of them known to exist. This particular Wagner card had been auctioned three times by Mastro (including once to hockey great

Wayne Gretzky) and was considered to be the highest-graded of all the known Wagner cards. But that was because Mastro had secretly trimmed the card—a fact that Thompson and O'Keeffe were able to uncover in all their reporting. Mastro repeatedly denied trimming the card right up until he was sentenced to 20 months in prison by a federal judge in Chicago in 2015 after pleading guilty to using phony bids to fraudulently inflate the price of his company's auction listings.

A year before I started looking into the corruption in the baseball memorabilia auction industry, I got a call from a source of mine in the Manhattan U.S. attorney's office. He told me the Internal Revenue Service was looking into the various autograph shows—card shows as they were called—that had mushroomed from the National Sports Collectors Convention in the early '80s and at which players were being paid tens of thousands dollars in cash for signing memorabilia. "They're after a lot of big-name players," my source said, "but one in particular you and your newspaper I'm sure will be interested in."

"Who's that?" I said.

"Darryl Strawberry."

Wow, I thought, *how much more could Darryl do to torpedo his career?*

He was 31 then, a long way from his heyday as the slugging star of the 1986 World Series champion New York Mets.

Ever since he bolted the Mets as a free agent for a five-year, $20.4 million deal with the Los Angeles Dodgers in 1990, Strawberry's career had spiraled downward amid a series of injuries and drugs, and according my source, he was facing serious jail time. Beginning with my initial story on June 20, 1993, in which I wrote that Strawberry "was the focus of a federal income tax evasion probe for allegedly failing to report thousands of dollars he earned signing balls, bats, cards, and other memorabilia," my source provided me with frequent exclusive updates as to how the probe was proceeding with various witness testimony right up to his indictment on December 9, 1994.

Strawberry eventually agreed to a plea deal on February 9, 1995, in which he was fined a substantial amount of money and sentenced to three months in prison, beginning March 15, to run concurrently with his 60-day drug suspension from baseball. I made a point of going to his sentencing hearing at the U.S. District Courthouse in White Plains, New York, though I was very much uncertain as to how he would react to seeing me there.

As he walked into the courtroom attired in a conservative dark blue suit with a multi-colored striped and flowered tie, he stopped briefly by the front row bench where I was seated with a couple of other sportswriters. "Hi, Bill," he said, "it's okay. I know you were only doing your job."

That was Strawberry, who was never one to blame anyone else for his troubles. I had always liked him when he was the toast of Shea Stadium with the Mets in the '80s and liked him even more after he turned his life around and had a terrific last hurrah as a World Series champion with the Yankees in 1999 before finding God and going into the business of saving lives as a drug counselor. He will always be a Hall of Fame person to me.

And for the record, Strawberry was not the only one caught up in the federal tax probe of the sports autograph and memorabilia business. In January of 1990, Pete Rose was fined $50,000 and sentenced to five months in jail for failing to report $345,967 in income from card shows, and in July 1995, Hall of Famers Willie McCovey and Duke Snider pled guilty to failing to report income from three days of signing at a 1989 memorabilia show in Atlantic City.

I made a habit of attending a lot of these card shows in the New York/New Jersey metropolitan area usually in the company of Halper, who was treated as much a celebrity as the players signing autographs. By the mid '90s, however, Halper had begun to slow down. Afflicted by severe diabetes that resulted in him having to wear a huge cumbersome boot on his foot, he knew he was going to have to dispense of his collection for estate purposes and in 1998 he signed a deal with Sotheby's to auction the bulk of it, and it wound up netting a total of $21.8 million over a seven-day period in September 1999.

But he had always wanted the Hall of Fame to have some of his most cherished items—he'd already donated one of his three T-206 Wagner cards to them—and in November 1998, a deal was reached in which Major League Baseball purchased 20 percent of his collection items for $7.5 million out of its central fund—roughly $266,000 per club—and donated them to the Hall of Fame.

To celebrate the occasion, there was a private reception at the Hall of Fame, and many of Halper's prized acquisitions were on display, including a 1919 Shoeless Joe Jackson uniform, which the disgraced slugger had purportedly worn in the fixed World Series that year, along with Jackson's famous "Black Betsy" bat; the Babe's famous polo coat; a trophy bat given to Hall of Fame manager Harry Wright in commemoration of the record winning streak of his 1868–70 Cincinnati Red Stockings; game-worn jerseys by Mickey Mantle, Cy Young, and Walter Johnson; and finally a trove of Ty Cobb memorabilia he'd obtained from Cobb's biographer, Al Stump, that included a 1920s Detroit Tigers Cobb uniform, a game-used Cobb bat, numerous Cobb-signed documents, and a hand-written 1946 diary in Cobb's signature green ink.

Halper had often talked with great delight about the stuff he was able to obtain from Stump, especially the set of

Cobb's dentures and the shotgun, which Stump told him Cobb's mother had used to shoot Cobb's father after he snuck through the rear window of their house in Royston, Georgia, on August 9, 1905. Understandably, the Hall of Fame passed on those two items.

At the reception Hall of Fame president Jane Clark announced there would be a special room off the Hall of Fame gallery devoted to Halper and his collection called "Memories of a Lifetime: The Barry Halper Collection" in which all of these items would be on display. But as Halper stood off to the side, justifiably beaming with pride, I got to talking to Ted Spencer, the Hall's curator whose job it was to make sure all these items were properly authenticated. In particular, I wondered, *Where were all those 19th century Orioles uniforms Halper had bought from Ollie O'Mara?* "They were all no good," Spencer said. "We sent them out to this forensics lab we use, and they were able to determine that the threads in those uniforms were from the '20s."

My heart sank.

My worst fears about so many of Halper's uniforms were now realized. How many more of them were fakes? A lot of them, according to Joshua Evans, founder of Leland's Auctions and a respected authenticator who upon visiting the Halper room at the Hall of Fame said he was appalled at how much stuff was no good. As it turned out, a few months after

the Halper room in the gallery opened, the Jackson jersey—
which Halper claimed he obtained from Jackson's relatives
while driving through Shoeless Joe's hometown of Greenville,
South Carolina—was also not authentic after Evans blew the
whistle on it, and tests conducted by the Hall's forensics firm
confirmed the White Sox logo on the front contained acrylic
coloring that was first created in 1941. It was thus removed
from the gallery along with the "Black Betsy" bat, which by
association was deemed suspect.

Unfortunately, this was not the worst of it. In 2010
William R. Cobb (no relation to Ty), who was a member of
the Society of American Baseball Research (SABR) as well as
the Board of Advisors of the Ty Cobb Museum in Royston,
wrote a scathing article for SABR in which he quoted Evans
extensively accusing Stump as being a complete fraud who
forged the supposed 1942 Cobb diary, along with all the
other signed Cobb documents. In addition William Cobb
debunked the Ty Cobb shotgun story, citing an August 11,
1905 article in *The Atlanta Journal* in which Cobb's mother,
Amanda, testified that she had shot her husband with a pistol.

What a mess. All of Evans' and William Cobb's charges
against Stump and the inauthenticity of all the items he
sold Halper were later confirmed by the FBI and had to
be removed from the Hall of Fame. All anybody knew now
was that Halper's reputation had been sullied forever, and for

that I felt terrible. His entire life he'd strived to be someone famous and a prominent and respected member of the baseball establishment. As all these revelations about the forged and fake memorabilia in Halper's collection came to light, I thought back to something Mastro had said to me in 1994: "The problem we have in this hobby is that so many dealers and collectors *want* this stuff to be good."

Of this I do know: in an industry full of swindlers and crooks, Halper was not one of them. He honestly believed all his stuff, for which he'd paid hundreds of thousands of dollars, was real. He was a good person, who raised tens of thousands of dollars for the St. Barnabas burn unit in Livingston, New Jersey, by having his baseball friends, Joe DiMaggio, Rose, etc., speak at fundraisers. Halper loved baseball like nobody I'd ever known—to the point where sadly he became prey to all of those who knew just how much he would pay for that passion.

CHAPTER EIGHT

STEINBRENNER AND THE UNMAKING OF A COMMISSIONER

I had my ups and downs with George Steinbrenner. During the '70s and through the mid '80s when the New York Yankees were always competing in spite of the constant Steinbrenner-created turmoil around them, I found his antics to mostly be amusing (and always great copy). Looking back, I was probably one of the few writers at the time who genuinely liked him. Whenever he would return my calls regarding Yankees business, he would often say, "The reason I return your calls, Madden, is because you're balanced in the way you report about me. Most of your colleagues aren't. That's all I ask: that you're balanced."

Of course, I never had any illusions about whatever access Steinbrenner granted me was because he was fond of me personally or because I was "balanced" in my reporting. Rather, my newspaper, the *Daily News*, had the second-largest circulation the country back then—1.7 million readers during the week and more than 2 million on Sundays. Steinbrenner always knew where he could get the most bang for his buck.

A great example of that was a mid-June tempest in 1983 with Steinbrenner and Billy Martin. The two had been feuding, as usual, with the team slumping at 29–30, and on a road trip to Milwaukee, Martin had defied Steinbrenner's orders to hold an off-day workout and two days later during a Saturday day game he spent the whole game sitting on a stool alongside the visiting team dugout, passing notes back and forth to his then-girlfriend Jill Guiver. This put the writers in a quandary as the game was being televised back in New York on WPIX. Did we make a big deal of this, risk incurring the wrath of Martin and stirring up a whole new brouhaha between him and Steinbrenner, even though it had nothing to do with the game? After a consultation in the press box, we made a pact that nobody would write about it, thus assuring our top priority—a nice relaxing night out for dinner and drinks in one of the best restaurant cities on the beat. Unfortunately, the next day I was told by Yankees public relations director Ken Nigro that Steinbrenner was aware of Martin's transgressions. "The Boss is really pissed," Nigro said. "You probably should call him before he calls somebody else. He might be firing Billy."

So I dutifully called Steinbrenner in New York, and Nigro was right. He was extremely pissed. "I'm not happy about a lot of things I'm hearing about Billy on the road," Steinbrenner said. "He promised me he was gonna have the team work out in Milwaukee and he didn't and he's fooling around with some woman, and the team is playing like shit. I think I'm gonna have to make a change."

"You're going to fire Billy?" I asked.

"He's giving me no choice," Steinbrenner snapped. "But I've got an idea and I want your thoughts. What do you think about Yogi as the manager?"

"Wow," I said. "That's an interesting one. But if you're gonna fire Billy, you're gonna have to replace him with someone equally or even more popular with the Yankee fans, and there's no more popular Yankee than Yogi Berra."

"That's what I'm thinking," Steinbrenner said.

"But you're aware that Yogi was already the Yankee manager in 1964, and they fired him?"

"That was 20 years ago," Steinbrenner said, "and I wasn't the owner. So what do you think?"

"If this is something you feel you have to do, what's not to like about Yogi? I think he'd be great," I said.

After hanging up I called my office in New York and told them I was writing a story that Steinbrenner was preparing to fire Martin and replace him with Berra. "Whoa!" my sports editor said. "Where did all this come from? Are you sure this is happening?"

"All I know is that's what Steinbrenner just told me."

So we ran the story on Page One the next day with a huge Bill Gallo cartoon of Berra under the headline of "Billy On The Brink" and in turn touched off a major shitstorm when the Yankees arrived in Cleveland the next day. Martin's agent, Eddie Sapir, also flew in to meet and try to smooth things over with Steinbrenner, who himself had flown in from New York. As I had always suspected he might, Steinbrenner relented on firing Martin, but he had achieved his purpose: another day of Page One off-the-field Yankees drama to divert everyone's attention from the Yankees' lousy on-the-field play. But I didn't feel Steinbrenner had used me to float this trial balloon about Berra managing the Yankees. It was a legitimate story. And after the season, he did fire Martin (for the third time) and replaced him with Berra.

I think I can speak for all the writers covering the team and say that we were privately delighted with the elevation of Berra from coach to manager. It meant a return to calm and normalcy from the constant Martin foibles, and we would now all be able to go to bed before the hotel bars closed. At the same time the writers—and almost all the Yankees players— were outraged when Steinbrenner fired Berra just 16 games into the 1985 season and brought back Martin for a fourth time. My everlasting vision of that awful day in Chicago when Steinbrenner ordered general manager Clyde King to inform Berra of his dismissal was the scene on the team bus at O'Hare International Airport where our chartered flight to Texas was waiting. When we boarded the bus at Comiskey Park, we were surprised to see Berra sitting in his accustomed manager's seat in the first row, but apparently he'd wanted to be with his team one last time. As we arrived at O'Hare, the bus suddenly stopped in front of the United Airlines terminal, and everyone watched in silence as Berra got off. For a minute the bus just stood there while we watched the lonely figure of Berra, the most decent and beloved of all Yankees, trudging slowly into the terminal, carrying his own luggage. The only sound on the bus was his son, Dale, staring out a window in the back, bawling uncontrollably. *No wonder,* I often thought, *why it took Berra 14 years to forgive Steinbrenner for this indignity.*

As an aside, I was on the receiving end of one of the great Yogi-isms of all time. It was April 1984, Berra's first year as Steinbrenner's manager, and we were on the second road trip of the season in Cleveland, staying at the Stouffer's Hotel. I went down to breakfast early, knowing that Berra was always the first person in the hotel coffee shop, and sure enough there he was, sitting all by himself. Upon spotting me, he waved me over to join him. He already had a plate of eggs, bacon, and toast in front of him. When the waitress came over and asked me what I wanted, I said: "Just an English muffin and coffee."

Berra and I sat for nearly an hour talking baseball and the status of the team, and when the waitress returned, I grabbed the check, which momentarily set me back. "Wow," I said, "$34? So much for breakfast in the hotel!"

Without missing a beat, Berra replied: "Oh, it must've been the English muffin. They got to import that."

More than anything, though, it was the heartless 1985 firing of Berra and yet another ridiculous recycling of Martin that convinced me Steinbrenner was simply not of a right mind. He could not comprehend having the highest payroll in baseball not producing sustained championships. So he flailed about, firing managers and general managers, issuing inflammatory statements railing against the umpires and the league officials, feuding with his players, making impetuous trades and ill-advised free-agent signings all to the detriment of the Yankees. He had become baseball's Public Enemy No. 1.

I thought maybe there was some hope Steinbrenner might ease off when in 1986 he hired his "favorite son" Lou Piniella as manager. He had always made no secret of his affection for Piniella, and my thought was he'd want to do everything he could to help Piniella succeed. But nothing changed. The team finished second with 90 wins in 1986 and fourth the following year—plagued both seasons by myriad injuries and aging, mediocre starting pitching, and Steinbrenner constantly carping at Piniella. And even when Steinbrenner lured Piniella back with a three-year contract in 1988 after yet another Martin implosion, they both quickly realized it just wasn't going to work between the two of them.

After 10 years of covering him as a player and then two-and-a-half years as manager, Piniella and I had become close friends. We had a lot of dinners on the road together, and after games the then-Manager Piniella would invariably seek out Moss Klein of *The Star-Ledger* and myself in the hotel bar to serve as sounding boards for his (off-the-record) complaints about Steinbrenner. Then one day in mid-September 1989, Piniella called me into his office and asked me to do him a favor. "I've heard from somebody in the commissioner's office that Steinbrenner has never filed my contract with them," he said. "I need you to poke around about this."

A couple of days later, I called Steinbrenner in Tampa, Florida, and asked him about the contract. "It's true I haven't filed it," he said, "but I have my reasons."

"Can I ask why?" I said.

"I'll tell you," Steinbrenner said, "but you can't write this because it's a very sensitive matter. During the course of going through our financial statements for the year, I discovered that Lou's been stealing from me."

"Stealing from you?" I said, consternated. "How could he be stealing from you?"

"There's an entry in the books listing $10,000 worth of Scandinavian furniture sent to Lou's home in New Jersey," Steinbrenner said. "I never authorized anything like that. If Lou's been stealing from me, I have to let him go. He's like a son to me, and I'm not going to prosecute him, but he has to go."

I hung up the phone shaking my head. This was just nuts. There had to be more to this story. And, sure enough as with Steinbrenner, there always was. The day after my phone conversation with Steinbrenner, he flew to New York for a meeting with his limited Yankees partners at Yankee Stadium. After the meeting I spotted one of the partners, Ed Rosenthal, standing by the batting cage. "What did The Boss have to say about our boy, Lou?" I asked him.

"He's gone," Rosenthal said. "Get ready for Dallas Green, sounds like the deal is done."

This is just great, I thought. *Not only do I not have a satisfactory answer for Piniella about his contract, but I now also have to write that he's being fired and replaced by Dallas Green, a Yankees outsider, who in 1980 had managed the Philadelphia Phillies to the world championship before moving over to the Chicago Cubs as general manager.* Needless to say when my story appeared on the front page of the *Daily News* the next day under the headline "Bronx Bombshell" and quoted sources saying Piniella would be replaced as manager by Green at the end of the season (but with no mention of any furniture), Piniella was quite upset. "Why couldn't you have waited to the end of the season to write this?" he asked me when I came into his office, as the paper lay on his desk.

"I wish I could have, Lou," I said. "But it couldn't wait. Too many people [who were at the meeting] knew about it, and it was gonna get out."

Much as I wanted to ask him about the furniture, he was in too foul a mood so I made my exit. But the story was out there now, and Steinbrenner had no choice but to call Piniella up to his office for a meeting of the minds. Once they'd had it out and they'd agreed to part ways, I felt I could ask Piniella about the furniture. "I'm just wondering," I asked him, "did he mention anything to you about any off-the-field issues that prompted him to hold off filing the contract with the commissioner's office?"

"Oh, you mean that bullshit about the furniture?" he shot back.

"Uh, yeah," I said, "that was something he brought up with me, but I wasn't about to write it until I talked to you."

"Do you believe that son of a bitch thought I was stealing furniture from him?" Piniella said as his voice began to rise. "I'll tell you what happened. When I came back to replace Billy and he gave me that three-year contract, part of the deal was I had to do this pre-game radio show—but for no extra pay. When I pointed out to him that all the other managers who did pre-game radio shows were compensated as much as $50,000, his answer was: 'You're already well compensated at $400,000 a year.' So I refused to do it."

That was when Arthur Adler, the Yankees vice president of business, stepped in and worked out a deal in which Piniella would be compensated for the radio show with advertisers' merchandise—and told him to have his wife, Anita, pick out what she wanted from a Scandinavian furniture catalogue.

As for me, I had now had it with Steinbrenner. I could not believe he could stoop so low as to try to justify firing Piniella by using me to suggest in the *Daily News* there was something far more sinister that led to his decision. It would be another two years before I spoke to him again.

During the period from 1981 and Steinbrenner's apology to the fans after the World Series to Piniella's firing in 1988, which precipitated the darkest period in the team's history, the one common denominator around the Yankees was Dave Winfield, who was named to eight straight All-Star Games, played all out all the time—and was hated by Steinbrenner. Actually, the seeds to Steinbrenner's lifelong rift with Winfield were sewn before the ink was even dry on the record 10-year contract for $1.4 million a year that Winfield signed with the Yankees in 1980. In addition, the contract called for a $1 million signing bonus for Winfield and a pledge of $3 million by Steinbrenner over 30 years for Winfield's foundation—along with an office at Yankee Stadium for Al Frohman, the agent who negotiated the deal.

The day after the Winfield deal was announced, Murray Chass of *The New York Times* reported further details of the contract, in particular a compounding cost-of-living elevator clause that could potentially make the deal worth nearly $25 million. The suggestion by Chass in the report was that Frohman had bamboozled Steinbrenner. It was left to Steinbrenner's perpetually under siege in-house counsel Ed Broderick to tell the media that he, not Steinbrenner, had been the one who negotiated the contract for the Yankees with the full understanding of the cost-of-living clause's potential value. But from that day on, Steinbrenner was engaged in mortal warfare with Frohman and the Winfield Foundation and by extension his new star slugger. And it certainly didn't help that in his first (and only) World Series for the Yankees in 1981, Winfield went 1-for-22.

For the next eight years, Steinbrenner and Frohman battled constantly over the Winfield Foundation, culminating in Frohman suing Steinbrenner for failure to make his required annual payments to the foundation and Steinbrenner filing a 25-page countersuit in U.S. District Court in Manhattan charging that the foundation with wasting tens of thousands of dollars on limousines and board meetings at expensive resorts and alleging that Winfield had past associations with gamblers to whom he had made "substantial loans."

Explosive as these charges were, the veteran Yankees beat reporters had a good idea where they had come from. For years we'd been getting late-night phone calls from a whiny-voiced guy named Howie Spira, who described himself as a gambler and a former employee at the Winfield Foundation who had reams of information revealing the foundation to be a fraud and Winfield to be "a bad guy who's destroyed my life." The writers, myself included, dismissed Spira as a crackpot and never followed up on any of his charges.

But Steinbrenner did.

It seemed Spira had been even more relentless in his vendetta against Winfield after he'd gotten ahold of Steinbrenner's home phone number in Tampa. At first Steinbrenner sloughed him off, but the more Spira dished to him about the foundation, the more it confirmed his own suspicions about behind-the-scenes chicanery going on with it, and he finally elected to use the information in his countersuit against Frohman. That was when Spira began pleading with Steinbrenner to pay him for the information, citing the fact that he was in deep debt to gamblers and feared for his life. Finally, and against the advice of his latest in-house Yankee counsel Bill Dowling, Steinbrenner agreed to pay Spira $40,000 to help take care of his debts with a foolhardy written stipulation that Spira "would not seek or create any publicity from this matter." It was foolhardy because Spira was incapable of shutting up and kept pestering Steinbrenner for more money. And all the while he was taping his phone conversations with the Yankees boss, including all the back and forth over the $40,000 payment, which in his desperation he then leaked to Richard Pienciak, the *Daily News'* chief investigative reporter.

Pienciak's subsequent bombshell front page story in the March 18, 1990 *Daily News* blew everything out in the open, and though Steinbrenner insisted he had nothing to hide and didn't care that the $40,000 payment to Spira had now become public, the new commissioner of baseball, Fay Vincent, thought otherwise. Vincent had been commissioner barely six months, having ascended to the job when Bart Giamatti, for whom he had served as deputy commissioner, suffered a fatal heart attack at age 51 on September 1, 1989. We, meaning all the writers and just about everyone in the game, loved Giamatti because he was a convivial, good-hearted and eminently decent fellow, a Yale scholar, a poet, and a hopeless romantic when it came to baseball. And even though he was also a chain smoker and overweight, there was much speculation that his heart attack could just as much been attributed to the enormous stress he'd been under during his three-month investigation of Pete Rose gambling on baseball that was spearheaded by Vincent and his special counsel, John Dowd.

In addition to being a close friend of Giamatti, for whom he negotiated his contract to be commissioner, Vincent was more than qualified for the job himself (maybe even more so than Giamatti, whose primary credentials had been being a former president of Yale who'd written a number of essays on his love of the game). Vincent, on the other hand, had a strong background in business and law, having previously been chairman of Columbia Pictures and vice president of Coca-Cola. He professed to have the same love of the game as Giamatti, and the finest hour of his commissionership may well have been just a month after being formally elected. He was confronted by the 1989 San Francisco earthquake that interrupted the World Series for 11 days.

Those were the worst two weeks of my career as a baseball writer, and I wasn't alone. Instead of covering the World Series, baseball's crown jewel event, we were all suddenly transitioned into news reporters covering the death and carnage in the streets of San Francisco. Periodically, we'd be doubling back to the St. Francis Hotel where Vincent was holding forth, conducting his daily candlelight press conferences while shepherding the game through this horrible tragedy. As Vincent later said, there was never a thought on his part that the World Series would be cancelled because "in a crisis there are some institutions that have to survive."

Once the World Series was able to be completed, Vincent was hailed by one and all in baseball for his calm, steady leadership. But at the same time, he was being continually confronted by pleas from Yankees fans, the New York media, and a large majority of owners and baseball officials to do something about his fellow Williams College alumnus, the menace that was Steinbrenner. The Pienciak revelation about Steinbrenner's $40,000 payment to Spira, purportedly for dirt on Winfield and his foundation, gave Vincent his opening for a full-blown investigation. And from the outset, it became clear Vincent and Dowd were going to be just as determined to bring down Steinbrenner as they had been with Rose.

So relentless had their efforts been to prove without a shadow of a doubt baseball's all-time hit king had repeatedly bet on baseball that they caused a major rift between Vincent and Giamatti that was never reported and never healed. One of Vincent and Dowd's key witnesses against Rose was a Franklin, Ohio, bookmaker named Ron Peters, who provided sworn testimony and copies of Rose's betting sheets. After Peters later pled guilty to cocaine distribution and tax evasion at his lawyer's request, Vincent and Dowd had Giamatti sign a letter to a U.S. District Judge in Ohio, Carl Rubin, praising Peters for his "candid, forthright, and truthful" cooperation in their Rose probe.

Rubin's response was to publicly castigate Giamatti for "having a vendetta" against Rose. And as I later learned from sources close to Giamatti, he was so furious at Vincent and Dowd after being publicly embarrassed by the letter, he planned to fire both of them. If that was indeed the case, Vincent and Giamatti weren't nearly the thick-as-thieves, close friends Vincent claimed they were when Giamatti died.

Meanwhile, in early May of 1990, Steinbrenner and his lawyer, Bob Gold, were called into the commissioner's office by Dowd to give a deposition about all that had gone down with the $40,000 payment to Spira. But a few days later when they were given a transcript of the deposition, they were outraged to discover Dowd had altered or deleted long passages of it. Since, as Vincent noted, it was merely an informal administrative hearing, there was nothing Steinbrenner's lawyers could do other than charging Dowd had acted in an unprofessional and unethical manner in his handling of the documents. Then after Dowd completed his report for the formal hearing with Steinbrenner, Vincent assured Claire Smith of *The New York Times*: "It is not my place nor is it the place of John Dowd to hide anything from George."

And yet he did just that, refusing Steinbrenner's lawyers' request for a copy of Dowd's report prior to the hearing, another blatant violation of Steinbrenner's due process rights. Vincent further told Smith that Steinbrenner would be allowed to call witnesses on his behalf to the hearing, which the commissioner later also reneged on, telling Steinbrenner's lawyers at the conclusion, "I have no intention of cross-examining any of the people that you might call as witnesses." One of those witnesses was to be Phillip C. Rizzuti, the court stenographer who'd told Steinbrenner's lawyers he'd been ordered by Dowd to alter Steinbrenner's sworn testimony.

Instead, with Steinbrenner's due process rights being trampled on all over the place, the hearing, which lasted two days, was mostly a one-on-one grilling of Steinbrenner by Vincent in which the commissioner continued hammering home the fact that the Yankees boss had done business with a known gambler in Spira. Clearly, Vincent was trying to inject the gambling element into the case since gambling on baseball was the game's No. 1 cardinal sin and carried a lifetime ban as the penalty.

It was a ridiculous stretch, but by now Steinbrenner's lawyers realized this was a kangaroo court. After three weeks of deliberation, Vincent handed down his 50-page decision on July 30, 1990, in which he declared he was suspending Steinbrenner for two years, concluding that Steinbrenner's $40,000 payment to Spira and "their undisclosed working relationship" constituted conduct not in the best interest of baseball. That was when Steinbrenner made the worst trade of his baseball career. Concerned the stigma of a suspension would jeopardize his position on the U.S. Olympic committee, he asked Vincent if there was an alternative punishment. "Actually, there is," Vincent said, "you could agree to go on the 'permanent ineligible' list" (or the equivalent to a lifetime ban).

Imagine Vincent's astonishment (and delight) when Steinbrenner said okay to this. Nobody could believe Steinbrenner had been so misguided, and Vincent was now the toast of baseball, having successfully rid the game of one of its most notorious miscreants. I was like most everyone around the game who had no sympathy for Steinbrenner. I still wasn't talking to him and I thought he could do everyone a favor now by just selling the Yankees.

It wasn't long, however, before Vincent became more and more emboldened with power, first incurring the wrath of a number of the more hawkish baseball owners by overstepping baseball's executive council and injecting himself in the stalled labor talks in 1990 with a number of suggestions to the players union in an attempt to end the spring training lockout. Vincent's growing power lust was later on full display in the summer of 1992 when he unilaterally attempted to force realignment on the National League by shifting four franchises, including the Chicago Cubs, to different divisions. It was a decision for which he was quickly rebuffed when the Cubs sued, and a federal judge ruled he had exceeded his authority.

But as the owners were becoming more and more disenchanted with Vincent, the decision that really sealed his doom—and exposed him as the total opposite of his friend Giamatti but rather the same sort of bully as

Steinbrenner—was his public reprimand of the "Yankee Three"—vice president Jack Lawn, GM Gene Michael, and manager Buck Showalter—for testifying at a players union grievance hearing on behalf of drug-plagued Yankees reliever Steve Howe. On December 19, 1991, Howe was arrested on cocaine possession charges in Kalispell, Montana, and even though he was able to avoid jail time by filing an Alford plea of no contest, he had already been previously suspended six times by baseball for drug-related offenses, and Vincent was determined to make an example of him by announcing he was suspending him indefinitely. The Players Association immediately filed a grievance to be heard in front of baseball arbiter George Nicolau, which Vincent sought to circumvent by unilaterally revoking baseball's rules of procedure. The rules of procedure were essentially baseball's bill of rights put in place by previous commissioners to establish protocol for investigations, hearings, and disputes.

When Vincent found out Lawn, Michael, and Showalter had testified at the hearing for Howe, he went ballistic and in an impulsive action that set off alarm bells all over baseball summoned the three of them to his office at 350 Park Avenue shortly before the start of a getaway day game against the Kansas City Royals at Yankee Stadium—and further told them they were not allowed to bring their attorneys with them. "I cannot understand why you three would voluntarily [they were actually subpoenaed] appear at a Players Association hearing without the consent of the commissioner and then at the hearing be critical of the commissioner's decision on Steve Howe," Vincent fumed, adding that as far as he was concerned they'd all effectively "tendered their resignations from baseball."

Shortly after the hearing, I was able to obtain a copy of Vincent's letter to the owners informing them of his intention to do away with the rules of procedure. It was as outrageous as his subsequent threats against Lawn, Michael, and Showalter. His reasoning, he said, was that the rules "had no practical benefit," and that recent lawsuits against the commissioner's office had "intentionally misinterpreted them" so he would hereby "proceed informally on a case-by-case basis." In other words, the commissioner should still have supreme and absolute power so as not to be overruled by judges or arbitrators. "That letter by Vincent really opened everyone's eyes," Chicago White Sox board chairman Jerry Reinsdorf told me.

And it also opened the door for Steinbrenner's attorneys, Arnold Burns and Randy Levine, to present their case in a 135-page report to the owners for Steinbrenner's reinstatement. In the report they cited all the examples of how Vincent had denied him due process. (It didn't hurt either that Steinbrenner also had won an extortion case against Spira, who was sentenced to 30 months in a federal penitentiary.) As Levine later told me: "Up until then I think most of the owners were glad George was gone, but once they read our report, they came to realize that what Vincent had done to him he could just as easily do to them."

After Vincent's threat to kick Lawn, Michael, and Showalter out of baseball, the Players Association announced its intentions of filing an unfair labor practices suit, charging Vincent with witness tampering. But before the suit went any further, Nicolau stepped in and—like the federal judge in the Cubs suit—slapped Vincent down with a stern warning to him not to take any action against the Yankee Three.

Sensing the walls closing in on him and aware that baseball's executive council was about to act on Steinbrenner's petition for re-instatement, Vincent called Arnold Burns to his office on July 23, 1992 and informed him he was ready to issue a reprieve that would allow the Yankees boss to assume active control of the Yankees on March 1, 1993. But it was too late. The owners were now more united than ever against him and on September 3 made that known with an 18–9 vote of no confidence in him. Five days later, Vincent reluctantly resigned.

It was Michael's lawyer, Bob Costello, who perhaps summed up best what led to the downfall of the man I came to call "the imperial commissioner." He said: "The word to describe Fay Vincent is 'hubris,' which means fatal arrogance. Look it up in the dictionary, and it's right there. Hubris: fatal arrogance. See: Fay Vincent."

Shortly before the start of spring training in 1993, I happened to be in Tampa conducting some interviews for a book project I was working on and staying at Steinbrenner's hotel, the Bay Harbor. Throughout his two-year exile from baseball, I had not seen nor talked to Steinbrenner. I just reported on all his legal wrangling with Vincent. But as all the evidence of Vincent's denial of due process toward him came to light, I began to take his side. This one day I had just finished having lunch in the Bay Harbor dining room and began walking up the long hallway to the front lobby when I spotted a figure coming toward me from the other end. It was kind of like the opening scene in *Gunsmoke*. "Is that you, Madden?" I heard him holler.

"I plead guilty," I shouted back.

"What are you doing in my hotel?" Steinbrenner said as he drew closer.

"Well, George, I'm in town working on a book project and I like staying here. Why? Are you going to throw me out?"

He was right in my face now and, as I stopped in my tracks, he suddenly grabbed my shoulders and said: "What ever happened to us, Billy?"

It was a strange greeting for which I had no immediate answer. I can only guess it was Steinbrenner's way of saying he appreciated the "balanced" way I had reported the holy war with Vincent that nearly destroyed him but instead wound up ending the reign of the imperial commissioner.

Through the years I would often run into Steinbrenner at Elaine's, the renowned uptown saloon/eatery and melting pot of actors, writers, politicians, mobsters, and assorted other New York characters. Elaine Kaufman was a den mother to us all. She loved the sportswriters and had a reserved table for us in the front of the place right across from the bar, where on Friday nights my *Daily News* colleague, sports media columnist Bob Raissman, and I would hold forth, never knowing what celebrity she was going to have sit with us.

But Kaufman was particularly close to Steinbrenner. She was part of his inner circle, omnipresent in his private box at Yankee Stadium for every Opening Day and every postseason game, always adorned with a stunning gold necklace that had a pendant from the 1977 Yankees world championship.

It was sometime in 2008 when another Elaine's regular, Levine, then the Yankees' president, was sitting at a table in the back with his wife, Mindy, and waved me over. "When are you gonna write a book about The Boss?" Levine asked.

By this time Steinbrenner's health was failing badly, and he'd become more and more reclusive. At the same time, there was a shroud of silence within the Yankees organization regarding his condition. "I've been thinking about it for a while, Randy," I said. "But none of his friends and associates and—certainly not your people—are gonna talk to me, especially while he's alive."

"Somebody's got to write the book on him," Levine said. "We've recently been approached by a couple of writers, but we've told them we won't cooperate with them. The book should be written by someone who knows him and will be fair and not do a hit job on him. You're the writer who knows him best. You should be the one who writes the book."

"Well, I'd love to do it," I said, "but how do I get all his friends and associates to talk to me?"

"Don't worry about that," Levine said. "I'll tell them it's okay to talk to you. If they ask, you can tell them that you have permission from the Yankees."

Thus began an exhaustive 15-month research and interview odyssey into the life and times of one of the most complex men I have ever known, in which the finish line kept moving on me. *Steinbrenner: The Last Lion of Baseball* was published in March 2010, and as I told my editor at Harper-Collins: "The hardest thing we're going to have with this book is convincing people it's nonfiction. Nobody is going to believe the way this man behaved for 50 years."

Steinbrenner was never aware I was doing the book, but I'd like to think he'd have considered it to be "balanced." He died July 13, 2010, at age 80 in Tampa, and the book immediately skyrocketed into the top 10 on *The New York Times* bestseller list. I'd been making the rounds of all the network and local talk radio and TV shows in New York who were all eulogizing Steinbrenner when I stopped at Elaine's to offer my condolences to her. She was sitting at a table in front and immediately waved me over. I sat down next to her and said how sorry I was about losing our friend when she suddenly hugged me around the neck and whispered in my ear: "Georgie did good by you, Billy."

For a moment that completely caught me off guard, but I knew what she meant. By dying when he did, Steinbrenner had made my book a runaway bestseller. We were both smiling and misty-eyed. "Only *you* could get away with saying that, Elaine," I said.

CHAPTER NINE

SCANDALS, CHEATERS, AND THE A-ROD FOLLIES

I t's been proclaimed by many famous people for decade after decade that baseball is the greatest game of all. I'm not at all sure if that's true anymore, but of this I am absolutely certain: it is the most *resilient* game of all, having survived a players-fixed World Series in 1919, an owners-cancelled World Series in 1994, a major drug scandal in 1985 that ensnared some of the game's biggest stars, and, most egregious of all, the scourge of steroids that obliterated some of its most sacred records and diminished sure shot first-ballot Hall of Famers Barry Bonds, Roger Clemens, and Alex Rodriguez from demi-gods to disgraced pariahs.

Looking back, it's amazing to me that for so long the first baseball commissioner Kenesaw Mountain Landis' leading role in ridding the game of gambling after suspending for life the eight Chicago White Sox players, who conspired to fix the 1919 World Series, completely overshadowed his likewise leading role in keeping the game segregated. It seems incomprehensible today that from 1900 to 1947 nobody seemed to care that Major League Baseball (and all the other pro sports for that matter) was all White. Nor did anyone seem to realize (or care) there was one man most responsible for keeping it that way (albeit with the owners' full complicity), and that man was Landis.

(It was partly for that reason in 2004 I decided to write my book *1954—The Year Willie Mays and the First Generation of Black Superstars Changed Major League Baseball Forever*, which detailed baseball's slow progress on integration and how seven years after Jackie Robinson broke the color line, half of baseball, including six of the eight American League teams, had still not brought a player of color to the majors!)

When the next big scandal to rock baseball, the September 1985 Pittsburgh drug trials, unfolded, I was spending way too many nights in bars monitoring and babysitting Billy Martin and trying to avoid becoming an alcoholic myself as the *Daily News'* New York Yankees beat writer. I didn't have a relationship with any of the big names in the scandal—most of them National Leaguers—who testified before a grand jury about their involvement with cocaine. Like everyone, however, I was very much disturbed by the lurid testimony from some of the players: Tim Raines admitted to keeping a vial of cocaine in his uniform pocket, which he revealed he snorted during games while avoiding head-first slides so as not to break it. And Keith Hernandez, whom I liked and respected for his honesty and baseball acumen, admitted he'd done cocaine for three years while adding he believed as much as 40 percent of the players in baseball were doing it.

At the dawn of the 1998 season, baseball was still recovering from the disastrous decision by Bud Selig and the owners in 1994 to cancel the World Series for the first time in history, precipitating a 232-day work stoppage because of their inability to reach a new labor deal with the players. Overall attendance plummeted 19.8 percent in 1995 and then had only very modest increases in '96 and '97. Like the emergence of Babe Ruth in 1920 electrified the game with his phenomenal 54 homers that served to erase the stain of the 1919 Black Sox, the baseball owners in 1998 were looking for something or someone to restore the passions of so many fans who still felt jilted by them.

They got it in the persons of Mark McGwire and Sammy Sosa, who engaged in a spirited (if improbable) summer-long pursuit of Roger Maris' longstanding record of 61 homers in a season. When McGwire broke Maris' record on September 8 and Sosa later tied him at 62 on September 13, baseball was once again the center of the sports universe. McGwire's and Sosa's home run feats were seemingly not to be believed, but in their efforts to explain it, the writers and pundits chalked it up to everything from juiced baseballs, an expansion year with an additional 25 to 30 previously minor league pitchers, and smaller ballparks. Everything except what turned out to be the real underlying factor, even though it was right there in front of us all.

Both McGwire, 34, and Sosa, 29, along with a whole lot of other major leaguers, had added considerable bulk to their frames in recent years, but that was largely attributed by the media to enhanced weight training in baseball. There were whispers about steroids but only whispers because few knew exactly how much they could improve performance, and reporters found themselves tip-toeing around the issue out of fear of libel suits. Besides after dying NFL defensive end Lyle Alzado blew the whistle in 1992 on the evil of steroids in *Sports Illustrated*, most people considered it a football issue.

On the final day of the '98 season with McGwire at 68 homers to Sosa's 66, I was sitting in the Busch Stadium press box in St. Louis with Hall of Fame director of public relations Jeff Idelson. I was there to report history, and Idelson, the future of Hall of Fame president, was there to retrieve whatever artifacts of that McGwire history he could to bring back to Cooperstown, one of which turned out to be my signed scoresheet. Both of us were astounded when McGwire proceeded to hit two more homers, seemingly with ease.

That's the way I wrote it: "Seventy. Who in their wildest dreams could have ever imagined it? How to digest the sheer magnitude of such a number? *And yet, there it is today, a number to stand for the ages—70 home runs by Mark McGwire, 10 more than The Babe, nine more than Maris, and you have to believe more than anyone will ever hit in a season unless they institute batting tees."*

We were Pollyannas. It was just too good a story. The only hint that something might be amiss in this glorious pursuit of the home run record was an August 22, 1998 story by Associated Press baseball writer Steve Wilstein, a former colleague of mine at UPI in the '70s, who reported that McGwire had a bottle of Androstenedione, a testosterone-producing drug that was available over the counter and legal in baseball but banned in the NFL, Olympics, and the NCAA, in his locker.

But instead of doing any further in-depth investigating into Androstenedione and its possible performance-enhancing effects, the media and baseball mostly scorned Wilstein for violating the sacred "what you see here, stays here" code of the clubhouse. The celebration went on, and in December *Sports Illustrated* named McGwire and Sosa co-Sportsmen of the Year and put them on their cover in white Roman togas with laurel wreaths on their heads. It took another four years for us to come to fully realize it was just too a good a story to be true.

It was in 2001 when steroids became an open discussion in baseball after a considerably bulked up Barry Bonds shattered McGwire's record by hitting 73 homers and winning the first of four straight National League MVP Awards. Witnessing this I realized how naïve I had been in extolling McGwire's feat of 70 homers in 1998. Before that, the only thing in which Bonds had ever led the league in was churlishness to the media, and it sickened me even more six years later when he continued his steroids-fueled rampage by breaking the all-time home run record of 755 by Hank Aaron, one of the classiest players I had ever known.

When it came to the steroids cheats, I was the hardest of hardliners among my fellow BBWAA (The Baseball Writers' Association of America) scribes as far as the Hall of Fame voting was concerned. I was once asked by one of the younger writers who worked with me at the *Daily News* (and who voted for Bonds) if I would ever change my mind on Bonds, and this was my reply: "If I ever did, when I go up to Cooperstown every July for the Hall of Fame inductions, I could never look Hank Aaron in the face."

The other argument for Bonds from his supporters—"Well, he was already a Hall of Famer before he started taking steroids"—is especially ludicrous, at least if you're taking into account the "sportsmanship/character/integrity" clause in the Baseball Writers' voting instructions. It was like saying Joe Jackson was a Hall of Famer until he agreed to get involved in a conspiracy to fix the World Series.

Meanwhile, in August 2000 the *Daily News* hired a woman named Teri Thompson from ESPN where she'd been a news editor for *SportsCenter* and their outlets. With the blessings of publisher Mort Zuckerman, she was given a free hand to create her own sports investigation team. Thompson, I quickly learned, had a natural skepticism about sports, and having previously worked as an editor at the *Daily News* from 1997 to 1998, she immediately set her sights on fleshing out everything that had gone on with McGwire and Sosa and just how pervasive steroids had become in baseball. One of the first things the *Daily News* I-Team was able to uncover was that as early as 1989–93 the FBI had conducted the first major federal investigation into illegal steroids distribution, code named Operation Equine, that eventually led to more than 70 convictions of steroids suppliers. In our own *Daily News* I-team steroids reporting, one of our sources was Greg Stejskal, the FBI agent who'd headed up their investigation, and he conceded Operation Equine would have been a much more sensational story if they'd been given resources to go after players, too.

It was left to Jose Canseco to provide the players' names. In February of 2005, Canseco, the 1988 American League MVP and McGwire's fellow Oakland A's "Bash Brother" who'd led the American League with 42 homers and 124 RBIs that year, blew baseball's burgeoning "dirty little secret" steroids scandal wide open with a sensational tell-all book *Juiced* in which he revealed among other things that he personally had injected

McGwire and Jason Giambi with steroids with the A's, as well as Rafael Palmeiro, Juan Gonzalez, and Ivan Rodriguez after he was traded to the Texas Rangers. Canseco also fingered Clemens as someone he personally aided in juicing.

Several months earlier, in October 2004, *San Francisco Chronicle* reporters Mark Fainaru-Wada and Lance Williams— who'd been out front in reporting on a federal investigation of a sports supplement company in the Bay Area (BALCO) and its founder Victor Conte for allegedly supplying high-profile athletes with a unique concoction of undetectable drugs— were the first to publicly link Bonds to steroids. Fainaru-Wada and Williams revealed they had obtained a secret audio conversation in which Bonds' trainer, Greg Anderson, admitted Bonds had been using steroids provided by Conte.

Along with the Canseco book, it was all out there then, and outraged as Selig and the owners may have been, they had no place to hide, especially after a U.S. House Government Reform Committee called everyone, baseball officials and players alike, to Washington for a hearing on March 17, 2005. Until then baseball officials had continued to profess no knowledge of a steroids issue in the game.

But a few days after the Canseco book came out, Stejskal told my colleague, Christian Red of the *Daily News* I-Team, that in 1994 he had personally warned MLB's security chief Kevin Hallinan that steroids were becoming a widespread problem in baseball and named names his drug dealers had given him. "I alerted MLB back at the time when we had the case that Canseco was a heavy user, and they should be aware of it," Stejskal said. "I spoke to people in their security office, and Kevin Hallinan was one of them."

Yet nothing had ever come of it.

Armed with that revelation, a month before the congressional hearing, the *Daily News* on February 15 ran a back page story with the big bold headline "They Knew," detailing how federal investigators as far back as 1994 had informed baseball of its steroids problem that involved Canseco and other high-profile players. I remember Thompson telling us how sure she was that baseball would vehemently deny the story, and she was right. Hallinan said flatly: "It did not happen. Not with this guy [Stejskal], not with anybody else."

It took of all people—McGwire—to confirm our story, along with another story we'd published days before the hearing detailing his own extensive steroids use in his damning evasive testimony at the hearing when he repeatedly responded to the lawmakers' questions about his steroids use with "I'm not here to talk about the past."

I find it hard to believe that Hallinan never told Selig of Stejskal's disclosures, but I can also understand why baseball had continued to operate with their heads in the sand on the steroids issue—even after *Sports Illustrated*'s Tom Verducci's alarming interview with Ken Caminiti in June 2002 in which the former National League MVP had admitted his own steroids use and the severe effects he was having from them while asserting: "It's no secret what's going on in baseball. At least half the guys are using steroids."

For one thing, until McGwire's testimony before Congress—despite the suspicions—there'd been no definitive proof that he and Sosa had used performance-enhancing drugs to shatter Maris' home run record, and baseball was going to protect that as long as it could. For another thing even after the Canseco book exposed so many big-name players as steroids users, Selig knew there was nothing he could do without the full cooperation of the players union, which only finally happened after he and union chief Don Fehr were lambasted by the lawmakers at the hearing. (Previously, the union had only agreed to a weak testing plan with minimal punishments after an anonymous random testing of 1,438 players in 2003 revealed more than 5 percent positive results.)

I was told by one of Selig's underlings in the commissioner's office that he left the hearing infuriated and screamed to his staff: "I am not going to take the fall for this! It's the union's fault we haven't been able to get a handle on this with a comprehensive drug testing agreement, and, by golly, we're going to get one now!" In the meantime he enlisted the services of George Mitchell, former U.S. senator from Maine, to conduct his own independent investigation of steroids in baseball.

As Mitchell went about his work, the steroids revelations in baseball kept on coming. On June 6, 2006, federal agents raided the Scottsdale, Arizona, home of former Yankees relief pitcher Jason Grimsley, seeking evidence that he had been a distributor of human growth hormone. Four months later numerous reports surfaced that Grimsley told investigators that his former Yankees teammates, Clemens and Andy Pettitte, used "athletic performance-enhancing drugs" and that 2002 American League MVP Miguel Tejada used anabolic steroids.

On December 13, 2007, Mitchell released the 409-page report of his 21-month investigation on steroids in baseball to a huge media throng at the Grand Hyatt Hotel on 42nd Street in Manhattan. We had been given a heads-up that some of the biggest names in baseball would be named in the report as connected to steroids in one way or another, and in fact there were 89 players altogether, including Bonds (103 times), Clemens (82 times) Pettitte, Tejada, Giambi, Canseco, David Justice, Lenny Dykstra, Gary Sheffield, Gonzalez, Ivan Rodriguez, Mo Vaughn, Chuck Knoblauch, Benito Santiago, and Todd Hundley. Also included: former Cy Young Award-winning closer Eric Gagne, who registered a record 84 consecutive saves from 2002 to 2004 but in 2012 admitted in his book he'd been taking steroids the whole time, "which was sufficient to ruin my health, tarnish my reputation, and throw a shadow over the extraordinary accomplishments of my career."

Because Mitchell did not have subpoena power, however, his investigation was limited in scope, and it was clear the most titillating aspects of it were largely based on the testimony of just two people—Kirk Rodomski, a New York Mets clubhouse attendant from 1985 to 1995 who in April 2007 pled guilty in U.S. district court to money laundering and illegal distribution of anabolic steroids and human growth hormone, and Clemens' strength and conditioning coach, Brian McNamee, who admitted to injecting Clemens with steroids in 1998 and continuing to provide him with performance-enhancing drugs through 2001. The day after Mitchell released his report, Canseco, whose name appeared 105 times in it, dismissed it as a slap on the hand. "The report proved nothing," he said. "It just proved what we already knew." And he was right.

There were also notable and suspicious omissions in it; that Mitchell, who at the time was on the Boston Red Sox board of directors, mentioned no Red Sox players in his report particularly raised eyebrows, especially after Manny Ramirez was later twice suspended by baseball for testing positive for steroids and, along with David Ortiz, was reported by *The New*

York Times in July 2009 to be among the 104 players who failed that anonymous random testing in 2003. In addition, there was no mention of any players from Selig's former team, the Milwaukee Brewers, particularly Ryan Braun, who later had a 2011 steroids suspension overturned on a technicality.

When Mitchell's press conference was over, Thompson and I were simultaneously shaking our heads and saying, "Is that all there is?" I wrote a column for the next day's *Daily News* in which I said Selig had made the right call in ordering a full-blown investigation of steroids in baseball, but he picked the wrong guy to do it: "Though Selig heaped praise on Mitchell as being a man of unimpeachable integrity and totally independent, a lot of people could not get past the fact the former senator is a director with the Red Sox, and it was inevitable this would be an issue if the Red Sox got off lightly in the investigation, which they did." I later added: "If Mitchell was going to rely so heavily on the feds-provided witnesses Radomski and McNamee to out Clemens, he had an obligation to interview anybody and everybody associated with other similar high-profile Hall of Fame caliber players who've had their names linked to steroids. Because he didn't, there are a lot of cheaters looking forward to having a very merry Christmas, having escaped the Mitchell Report, and more than a handful now are breathing easier about being elected to the Hall of Fame under false pretenses because nobody was able to dig up any hard evidence against them."

Who was I talking about? Once again, it was left to Canseco to bring forth the elephant in the room in an interview with the FOX Business Network in which he said: "I saw the list of players, and there are definitely a lot of players missing...All I can say is the Mitchell Report is incomplete. I can't believe Alex Rodriguez's name was not in the report." (Indeed, A-Rod had also been mentioned in the 2009 report by *The New York Times* as one of the players who'd failed that 2003 anonymous test.)

Interestingly, a month before Mitchell's report was released, A-Rod agreed to terms with the Yankees on a new 10-year, $275 million contract that was the result of his unceremonious opt-out of his previous 10-year, $252 million deal he'd signed with Texas in 2000. His decision to announce the opt out in the eighth inning of Game Four of the 2007 World Series only further infuriated Selig and all the other MLB officials. When he realized what a furor he had caused, A-Rod weakly admitted the opt-out "was not handled well."

But as angry as the Yankees may have been at this blatant greed grab on the part of A-Rod and his agent Scott Boras, opting out of what was already the richest contract in baseball history—and even though they knew no other team in baseball would venture anywhere close to that $10-year, $252 million deal—they nevertheless capitulated when A-Rod came crawling back to them after enlisting the help of Goldman Sachs managing director Gerald Cardinale, who was also on the Yankees' YES Network board, to mend fences.

I could never understand why the Yankees threw in the extra $23 million on top of what was already an obscene contract that would now take A-Rod to age 42 when he had zero leverage. Their reasoning was he was still only 32, had just become the youngest player to surpass 500 homers, and they figured they could recoup a lot of that money by joint marketing deals and attaching their brand to his anticipated pursuit of Bonds' all-time home run record of 762. After all, Bonds' record was dirty, and nobody was taking it seriously. In A-Rod the Yankees would have the one "clean" all-time home run champion. It was an investment worth making, they thought, until it wasn't—when it became the biggest boondoggle in Yankees history. Barely two years into the contract, A-Rod's clean home run champion stock was worthless.

The decline of A-Rod began in the spring of 2009. His public image had already started to take a hit after his wife, Cynthia, had filed for divorce, charging him with infidelity amid published reports that he'd had an affair with Madonna. But then his secret steroids life came crashing down on top of him with a February 7 bombshell report by *Sports Illustrated*'s Selena Roberts who claimed in an excerpt from her forthcoming biography of Rodriguez that he'd indeed been one of the 104 players who'd come up positive in that 2003 anonymous MLB testing program.

He could have tried to brush off Roberts' *SI* report as more unsubstantiated rumors, but he knew the truth was closing in on him, and the Yankee brass ordered him to hold a press conference at George M. Steinbrenner Field where he finally came clean. Yes, he had taken steroids, he said, which had been procured for him by his cousin, Yuri Sucart, from the Dominican Republic. But it was only for his three seasons in Texas from 2001 to 2003, he insisted (not coincidentally the best three years of his career when he led the American League in homers in all three with 52, 57, and 47 and won the AL MVP in '03). "When I arrived in Texas, I felt enormous pressure. I had all the weight of the world on me [because of the contract] and I needed to perform," he said. "Back then [baseball] was a different culture. It was loose. I was young. I was stupid. I did take banned substances and for that am very sorry. You wanna throw them out? Fine, throw them out. It was only those three years in Texas."

For their part, the Yankees issued a statement of tacit support which said in part: "We urged Alex to be completely open, honest, and forthcoming in addressing his use of performance-enhancing drugs. We take him at his word that he was."

Ah, if only. A couple of days later, the *Daily News* I-Team obtained a copy of Roberts' book and published further details in it, among which she claimed A-Rod did not stop using steroids after he was traded to the Yankees and that he'd been using as far back as high school.

Just what the Yankees needed to hear. Compounding all this distressing steroids news, in early March A-Rod announced he was going to have to undergo labrum surgery on his right hip. It was an injury that seemingly came out of nowhere. Was it steroids related? No one could say, but A-Rod did not return to the field until May 8 and he was never the same player for the rest of his career.

I had no sympathy for the Yankees. In my May 6, 2009 *Daily News* column I wrote: "Beyond the crazy contracts, beyond the steroids, beyond the 'A-Fraud' revelations in Joe Torre's book, beyond the hip, there's always going to be something else with A-Rod, and none of it is ever good for the Yankees."

If only I'd known the worst was yet to come.

On August 19, 2012, our *Daily News* I-Team broke a sensational story that Melky Cabrera, who'd been A-Rod's teammate on the Yankees from 2005 to 2009, had undertaken a bizarre attempt to avoid a 50-game steroids suspension from baseball by creating, along with an employee of his agents, a fictitious website and a nonexistent product all designed to prove he inadvertently took a banned substance that caused his positive test. But instead of exonerating Cabrera, the Internet stunt trapped him in a web of lies, and what could have been a simple suspension now attracted further attention from MLB investigators and the Players Association.

As we pointed out in our story, Cabrera was hoping to repeat the success of Brewers outfielder Braun, the 2011 American League MVP, who earlier in 2012 escaped a 50-game steroids suspension by raising doubts about the collection and storage of his sample.

Ever since hitting the ground running in 2000, Thompson and her I-Team bloodhounds had been all over the BALCO scandal and later with bevy of government sources and those close to Clemens led the damning coverage of the Rocket's steroids offenses, which they later incorporated into a book, *American Icon—The Fall of Roger Clemens and the Rise of Steroids in America's Pastime.*

In the aftermath of the BALCO scandal, Conte was sentenced to four months in a federal correctional institute and four months of house arrest after pleading guilty to one count of conspiracy to distribute steroids. He returned from his brief incarceration to run his other—legal—supplements company, Scientific Nutrition for Advance Conditioning, and became a prominent anti-doping advocate. He also became a valuable resource for the I-Team—both from an educational standpoint on steroids and for his inner knowledge of steroids still going on in baseball.

By late January 2013, our I-Team was working on a story linking A-Rod to an anti-aging clinic in south Florida called Biogenesis of America operated by a man named Anthony Bosch, which had been distributing and administering steroids to a number of major league players. On January 26 Thompson, Red, Michael O'Keefe, and myself reported that the Drug Enforcement Agency and Florida authorities were investigating Bosch, who we further reported had been advising A-Rod on nutrition, supplements, and blood analysis for the possible illegal distribution of performance enhancing drugs.

A few days after our story, the *Miami New Times* broke the Biogenesis scandal wide open after having obtained what they termed "an extraordinary batch of records" that were stolen from the Biogenesis clinic in Coral Gables, Florida, by a disgruntled employee of Bosch's. The documents included sales records of performance-enhancing drugs and Bosch's diaries of how and when he personally administered steroids to his clients, who included A-Rod, Cabrera, Braun, Nelson Cruz, Yasmani Grandal, and Bartolo Colon.

Conte had told Thompson of A-Rod's connection to Bosch. In an on-the-record interview with Thompson and O'Keeffe, Conte related that in May 2012 A-Rod and former star NFL linebacker and admitted BALCO steroids casualty Bill Romanowski had showed up uninvited on his doorstep to discuss legal products that could give Rodriguez an edge. A-Rod told Conte of his relationship with Bosch, who he referred to as his "nutrition guy," and later arranged a couple of telephone calls between Conte and Bosch to talk about A-Rod's nutrition regimen.

The Bosch doping documents were suddenly being seen as the Holy Grail for MLB, presumably the irrefutable evidence of steroids use by some of its biggest stars, most notably Alex Rodriguez, who by this time had become Selig's white whale. Though even further damaging to baseball's image, the Biogenesis scandal had also become the vehicle for Selig to seize his modern-day Landis moment as the savior who cleaned up the game from the scourge of steroids.

Until then, he'd been frustrated by the fact there'd been nothing he could do about Bonds and Clemens since neither of them had ever failed a steroids test. He was especially repulsed at Bonds for breaking Aaron's all-time home run record of 755. Selig idolized Aaron, who began and ended his career in Milwaukee, and he could barely contain his contempt for Bonds when he twice had to present him with the Hank Aaron Award, which he'd created, to honor the best hitter in the game. "Bud wants all of these guys," one of

Selig's lieutenants told me after the *New Times* story broke, "but no one more than A-Rod. He's the big fish now."

As such, Selig ordered his underlings to get those Bosch documents no matter what the cost. According to the book *Baseball Cop* by former MLB Department of Investigations member Eddie Dominguez (written with Red and Thompson), that cost wound up being $100,000 in cash stuffed in a brown paper bag and handed over by the MLB investigation team to a sinister character who identified himself only as "Just Bobby" at the Cosmos Diner in Pompano Beach, Florida. I never quite understood how MLB was able to escape federal scrutiny for buying stolen documents with a $100,000 in cash in a brown paper bag, but I guess they are able to do whatever they want as long as it's for "the good of the game."

And Selig certainly did exercise his good of the game powers once he had all the evidence he needed, which also included sworn testimony from his star witness, Bosch. On August 5, 2013, he meted out 50-game suspensions to 12 of the players in Bosch's doping records, plus 65 games for Braun and a whopping 211 games for A-Rod. (A side note here: Braun later called Thompson to apologize for calling our story of his original steroids bust "bullshit.") Although the players all had the right to appeal their suspensions under the MLB collective bargaining agreement, none of them did—another victory for Selig.

The one exception was A-Rod, who proclaimed his innocence and vowed to fight. So, satisfied as he might have been to have hooked his white whale, it would take a while longer—and whole lot more of grief—before Selig was able to finally reel him in. Two days after Selig handed down the suspensions, the Players Association announced they were filing a grievance on A-Rod's behalf to go before the baseball arbitrator Fredric Horowitz. "There is nothing about this that has been easy," A-Rod told reporters in Chicago, where the Yankees were playing. "We're here now. I'm a human being. I am fighting for my life. If I don't defend myself, no one else will."

He was right about that.

Upon enlisting the services of the notoriously litigious high-stakes criminal attorney Joe Tacopina, A-Rod went on a lawsuit rampage in an effort to get his suspension overturned. The first salvo to be fired by Tacopina was his accusation to *The New York Times* that the Yankees and team president Randy Levine were conspiring with Selig to drive A-Rod out of baseball so they could negate the remaining $85 million of his $275 million contract. From there it got even uglier. On October 4 A-Rod sued MLB, charging that they had paid Bosch a total of $5 million in monthly installments to buy his cooperation while also citing the shady "brown paper bag cash transaction" for the stolen Biogenesis documents.

When it came time for A-Rod to plead his case before Horowitz, he barely made it. In the middle of the session, when he learned Horowitz would not be calling Selig to testify, he abruptly stormed out, reportedly shouting "this is bullshit!" without offering any testimony on his own behalf. Instead he took his case to the air waves, telling WFAN's Mike Francesa, his only supporter, "I shouldn't serve one inning" and continued to deny he ever did steroids beyond those three years in Texas.

Francesa, for some reason, was a borderline fanatic in his lonely and curious defense of A-Rod. Back in August, right after Selig announced his 211-game suspension of A-Rod, Francesa invited me on his show for what I quickly realized was his opportunity to vent about the *Daily News* I-Team's relentless (in his words) negative coverage of A-Rod. Why, Francesa repeatedly asked me, was A-Rod being treated so much worse by the *Daily News* than all of the other alleged or admitted steroids users? The interview pretty much went downhill from there:

Francesa: "Why has everbody made this all about A-Rod and nobody else? If it's about cleaning up the game, why is A-Rod being singled out here?"

Me: "Because he's the biggest offender. Plain and simple. Look at the suspension."

Francesa: "What about the guys you don't know about? How come your investigative team doesn't care about the other 100 names on that [2003] list that have never been made public? If you're going to clean up the game, why not start there?"

Me: "Well, how do you suggest we do that?"

Francesa: "Well, who's ever gone about doing that? How come the only name that got leaked was A-Rod's?"

Me: "There was more than one name."

Francesa: "Oh yeah? Who else?"

Me: "For one, David Ortiz."

Francesa: "Yeah, who denied it. No one says a word to David Ortiz. My point is: why is it all about A-Rod?"

Me: "Because right now in this Biogenesis case, he was the leader of the pack down there. And he's the guy Major League Baseball has the most evidence on."

Francesa: "What can you tell me that A-Rod has done other than use steroids? We know there have been hundreds of guys who have used steroids. What made A-Rod to the point where you have called him the Whitey Bulger of baseball?"

That was in reference to a couple of my columns where I had compared A-Rod to the notorious Boston organized crime boss who was No. 2 on the FBI's Most Wanted list for years. On that one I conceded to Francesa, such a comparison may have been a little over the top. I sat there for another 10 to 15 minutes listening to Francesa rant on about A-Rod having done nothing wrong. I kept to myself all I knew about the extensive Bosch doping journals. At the same time, I was frankly surprised Francesa had allowed himself to go so far out on a limb and risk his reputation on a proven liar like A-Rod.

On January 11, 2014, Horowitz issued his decision. The good news for A-Rod was that the arbitrator reduced his suspension from the 211 games. The bad news was that he would be banned for the entire 2014 season and postseason, costing him approximately $25 million in forfeited salary. Considering A-Rod had been a multiple steroids offender and a serial liar, a lot of people, myself included, were surprised Selig didn't give him the "Full Monty" Judge Landis lifetime ban for his transgressions against baseball. In retrospect, Selig was probably right to restrain himself from hammering A-Rod with the maximum sentence because it gave Horowitz wiggle room to levy just as harsh a penalty, and it would also be viewed as fair.

Of course, A-Rod didn't see it that way. Two days after Horowitz issued his opinion, A-Rod announced he was suing both MLB, as well as the Players Association, which he maintained "completely abdicated its responsibility to protect his rights." But once again, he'd blundered. By filing the lawsuits, it unsealed Horowitz's entire 34-page report, which was both detailed and devastating, including the shocking disclosure that A-Rod "attempted to induce Bosch to sign a sworn statement on May 31 saying he never supplied the player."

To me, that sounded a whole lot like an additional obstruction of justice charge against A-Rod. For a blessed 2014 season, A-Rod disappeared from view, and we could all go back to writing about baseball. As I wrote in my February 8, 2014 column right before spring training was to begin: "One of the ugliest chapters in baseball history is finally over, and out of it Rob Manfred, commissioner Bud Selig's drug sheriff, emerges as the biggest winner, if only slightly bigger than A-Rod's lawyers, who played to his vanity, gave him terrible advice, made a fortune off him, and doomed him to being the baseball pariah he will quickly discover he's become."

Just weeks after giving up his legal fights, A-Rod admitted to federal investigators that he had paid $12,000 a month to Bosch for steroids and other performance-enhancing drugs.

A final measure of satisfaction for Selig and Manfred was the BBWAA's rejection of A-Rod, Bonds, Clemens, Sosa, and McGwire for the Hall of Fame. I would have also thought this entire sordid A-Rod episode, especially his scorched earth crusade against MLB and the Players Association, would have sufficiently rendered him persona non grata in baseball for the rest of his life. Our *Daily News* I-Team members were right there in the middle of all of that, so imagine my surprise when

Selig and Manfred expressed no opposition to FOX Sports hiring A-Rod as a full-time TV analyst in 2017 or then a year later when ESPN hired him to be the lead analyst on *Sunday Night Baseball.*

I found myself shaking my head in consternation as to how the man, who Selig and Manfred went to such lengths to convict as the most grievous steroids cheat of them all, wound up as one of the primo faces of baseball only three years later. It was as if those five years of all those A-Rod lies and legal assaults on the baseball establishment had never happened.

CHAPTER TEN

THE ANALYTICS MYTH SPINNERS

"Any fool can make something complicated.
It takes a genius to make it simple."

—*Woody Guthrie, singer/songwriter*

Allow me, if you will, to assume the position of the grumpy fossil on the front porch hollering at the armies of analytics geeks, who have invaded baseball, to get the hell off my lawn. I'm not here to talk about xFIP, UZR, WPA, BABIP, OAA, xBA, wOBA, WRC+, Sprint Speed, or any of the other new-age metrics introduced into the baseball lexicon since Major League Baseball's implementation of Statcast in 2015 with its cameras in every nook and cranny of all 30 ballparks tracking the movement of baseballs everywhere from pitching, hitting, and throwing. Because like for most every baseball fan over the age of 50, these formulas are far too complicated for me to go into here and try to explain why it's a waste of energy and why for the most part experienced scouts and pitching coaches have always been able to see it with their own eyes anyway.

Prime examples: exit velocity and spin rates. With the advent of Statcast, exit velo, the measurement of how quickly baseballs leave the ballpark and which batters hit the balls hardest (see also: barrels), is the stat that quickly became the rage of all the analytically-embedded general managers. It's become so popular that many clubs now flash exit velo on the scoreboard along with the measurements of home runs. Whenever I'd hear baseball execs exalt about exit velo, I was reminded of how many times I'd hear people say of Hank Aaron, Willie McCovey, Willie Stargell, George Brett, Edgar Martinez, Reggie Jackson, and so many other Hall of Fame hitters (not to mention the notable steroids cheats Mark McGwire and Barry Bonds): "The ball just sounds different coming off his bat." So when I checked the hitters with highest exit velo averages for 2023, imagine my surprise to see Aaron Judge, Ronald Acuna Jr., and Shohei Ohtani rank first, second, and third.

The exit velo merely confirmed what we could see with our own eyes (or even hear). The best hitters in baseball hit the ball the hardest. *Duh?* Nice to know, I guess, but how does this help you win games? What was particularly interesting, however, was the presence of Giancarlo Stanton ranking eighth with an exit velo of 93.3 if only that it made me stop and think: *What good is a 93.3 exit velo when you hit .191 with 124 strikeouts in 415 plate appearances?* I suppose the real value of exit velo is that it's another measurement to separate the good hitters from the weak hitters.

At the same time, spin rates, which are essentially the measurement of revolutions per minute of the baseballs from the time they leave the pitcher's hand to when they reach the catcher's glove, have become the other favorite stat of the new-age analytics authorities, though nothing is new about them ever since it was determined Sandy Koufax's curveball had 13 revolutions on it from the time it left his hand to the time it landed in the catcher's glove. "What's new is that with Statcast and Trackman, we can now get an actual reading on spin rates," said a longtime baseball scout and pitching coach (who asked not to be identified for fear of losing his job). "But all the great pitching coaches—Mel Stottlemyre, Johnny Sain, Ray Miller, Roger Craig, Leo Mazzone, on and on—could tell spin rates just by watching the pitchers and then the batters' reactions. We've just added another layer of people analyzing pitchers who have only these spin rate numbers from Statcast to fall back on."

And what does it all mean? As my friend, Hall of Famer Jim Kaat, explained to me one time with a wry smile on his face: "It's interesting that they measure spin rates on revolutions of the ball per minute, but show me a baseball that stays in the air for a minute! They can measure all they want, but I know I had a much different spin rate pitching to a hitter in the eighth inning with two on than in the second inning with nobody on."

"In the end it all comes down to feel," the longtime scout said. "You can teach pitchers little things like altering their grips, but if they have it, they have it. You wanna know the one thing that can make a significant difference in spin rates? Sticky stuff!"

Baseball has nevertheless become obsessed with velo—and in my opinion to the detriment of pitchers, especially in the youth leagues where kids are pushed to throw as hard as they can if they want those big bonuses. More often than not, they then wind up with Tommy John elbow surgery in their 20s or earlier. Tom Seaver, who I'd say was a pretty good authority on the subject, would often tell me there are three principal ingredients to pitching: velocity, control, and movement, and that velocity was by far the least important of the three.

Of course, Seaver was speaking from the standpoint of the starting pitchers who have since been pretty much emasculated by analytics. It's a whole different game from when Seaver pitched, starting with one of the main tenets of analytics, which is not to let your starting pitcher face the starting lineup a third time around. I get it that the stats back up the fact that starting pitchers begin to lose their effectiveness the deeper they get into the game, but what the analytics can't show is the individual pitcher's makeup—not to mention the game circumstances. The third time around the lineup is a theory that should especially be viewed with caution in the postseason, where every out is precious, and in do-or-die situations, you should want your best pitcher to get them—as Tampa Bay Rays manager Kevin Cash in 2020 and Toronto

Blue Jays manager John Schneider in 2023 learned much to their detriment by removing their best pitchers, both of whom were pitching their asses off, to follow the analytics creed.

It happened with Cash in the sixth game of 2020 World Series when he pulled his ace, Blake Snell, who clung to a 1–0 lead, with one out in the sixth inning after just 73 pitches that included nine strikeouts. And then in the 2023 wild-card series, Schneider took out Jose Berrios, who was dominating the Minnesota Twins, in the fourth inning of a scoreless game after just 47 pitches. In both cases the bullpens promptly gave up the eventual winning runs, and the Rays' and Jays' seasons were over.

I don't know why they even bother listing the probable pitchers for a game anymore. A Gerrit Cole versus Justin Verlander matchup might look like the makings of a great pitchers' duel, but the chances are good neither will be around to get the decision—as opposed to a Seaver–Steve Carlton or Bob Gibson matchup of my youth when I knew I was in for a treat, watching them battle each other all the way to the ninth inning and sometimes beyond.

The analytics have turned it into a bullpen game today with velo being the driving force. The vast majority of the highest velo pitchers being signed by clubs today—especially the ones from Latin America, where baseball is less organized—are quickly consigned to the bullpen with the understanding that when they get to the big leagues their job will be to go into the game (when it starts, of course, after the fifth inning) and throw as hard as they can for one inning. All the good teams have at least three of these guys. At the same time, the starting pitchers coming out of high school and college—if it's deemed they should remain starters—are immediately put on pitch counts and told not to worry about pitching beyond the fifth inning. As a result, workhorse starters like Seaver are fast becoming dinosaurs.

On a 100-degree day in August 2017, Seaver and I were sitting on a couple of lawn chairs nestled under the Douglas firs at the far end of his vineyard in Calistoga, California, talking about the finer points of making wine, when he suddenly went off about what analytics was doing to his previous craft. "It just bugs the hell out of me what they're doing to starting pitchers now," he said. "Bugs the hell out Gibson. Bugs the hell out of Marichal. Bugs the hell out of Sandy. Bugs the hell out of all of us. Pulling these kids out of games after five, six innings? These kids aren't being given a chance to learn how to pitch. They don't know what they're missing and they're afraid to speak up. Look, I'm not there. I'm a farmer now, but I'll never understand having a computer making the decision about how many innings they're going to pitch. It's all about pitch counts. A hundred pitches and you're out of there!"

"What was your pitch count max?" I asked him.

"I had my own pitch count, around 135," said Seaver, who topped 200 innings in a season 16 times. "But during a game, I knew how to save pitches for when I needed them in the eighth and ninth innings. I wasn't going to waste pitches on the No. 9 hitter. These kids aren't taught that today. It's all about throwing as hard as you can for as long as you can. I feel for these pitchers today. I think they have the heart and the guts, but they just won't let them out of the corral!"

In 2014 there were 34 pitchers in the majors who logged 200 or more innings. A year later that number was down to 28, then 15 in 2016–17 and '19. Following the pandemic-shortened 2020 season, the 200-inning pitchers had dropped to single digits. At the same time, the MLB average of innings per game for starting pitchers had dropped a full inning—from six in 2014 to five in 2023.

So much for the notion that analytics was going to save the owners millions. Certainly not when it comes to starting pitchers. Now that baseball has created this whole new generation of five-inning starters, teams have become desperate for those rare top-of-the-rotation workhorses like Verlander, Max Scherzer, and Gerrit Cole, who made $43 million, $43 million, and $36 million, respectively, in 2023. Never was that desperation more evident than the 2023 offseason when the Los Angeles Dodgers forked over $325 million to Yoshinobu

Yamamoto, a perceived No. 1 starter from Japan who'd never thrown a single pitch in the major leagues, and another $135 million to oft-injured Tyler Glasnow, who'd never thrown over 150 innings in his career. As much as Seaver decried the analytics-driven debilitation of starting pitching, I wonder what he would have thought about Scherzer, one of the dwindling bona fide top-of-the-rotation innings-eaters like himself, being paid by the owners as much as $13,000 a pitch?

It's nuts.

Indeed, I never cease to be amazed at the naivete (or is it just stupidity?) on the baseball owners' part when it comes to determining a player's worth. The analytics geeks created a complicated formula for them—WAR or wins above replacement. Simplistically put, it establishes a supposed comprehensive value on every player above an imaginary replacement player from the minor leagues.

There are a number of different stats incorporated into WAR—doubles, triples, homers, walks, on-base percentage among them for hitters and strikeouts and innings pitched for pitchers. But it does not include runs, RBIs, and sacrifice flies or pitchers' wins because all of those stats require the help of teammates. Similarly, batting average is omitted from WAR because it does not include walks. For the record, if a player hits a game-winning sacrifice fly in the bottom of the ninth inning, his WAR will go down.

The WARmongers, as I call them, love walks and hate singles. But after years of being undervalued, walks may have now become a bit overvalued thanks to WAR. (For example, which is more important: Rickey Henderson leading off the game with a walk, which could very well lead to a run, or the No. 5 hitter being walked semi-intentionally to get to the weaker-hitting No. 6 hitter?) By contrast they disdain singles, even though singles put the ball in play, but have no problem with hitters striking out, which they consider just another kind of out. The owners love WAR (even if they can't comprehend it) because it wraps players into a neat all-encompassing value for them that also includes defense and baserunning, and MLB has recognized it as an official stat. But I know I am hardly alone in maintaining WAR may be the biggest analytical myth of them all.

How can I say such a thing? Well, let me submit what's *not* included in WAR. First and foremost, there's a player's makeup. You can't measure that, even though it may be the most important attribute of any player. Then there's clutch hitting (again because it depends too much on a player's teammates and is not a repeatable stat). WAR is ignorant of game situations and assumes the player goes up to the plate swinging for a home run with the score 13–1 every time as opposed to runners on base with the score tied in the ninth inning. Players are not robots. They're all trying to win and they're not trying to do the same thing in every situation.

The problem with WAR is everything about it is predicated on prediction and what *should* have happened in the game. I'm especially intrigued by how they factor defense into it. Obviously, it's easy to gauge a player's range just by watching him over a period of time. But what about instincts? Double-play pivots? Relays? Positioning? Amazingly, the analytics brigade has been able to take WAR back to the beginning of baseball time, though I'll be darned if I know how they've been able to factor in Napoleon Lajoie's defense in 1906.

WAR is a stat for the lazy. It's a stat for computer nerds sitting in an office poring over all these metrics and formulas without having to actually go to a ballpark and see the players in person or talk to their managers or coaches. The reason the owners like WAR so much is because, even though they have no idea what it is, they can talk the talk about it and feel like experts.

Here's all you have to know about the absurdity of WAR. In Baseball Reference's all-time top 100 players in WAR, Wade Boggs is ranked 43rd with a 91.4 wins above replacement. Now I loved Boggsie, who was a terrific hitter with five batting titles, an average defender at third base, and a fun guy, and I suppose his high-ranking WAR can be mostly attributed to his exceptionally high on-base percentage

(.415, ranked 27th all time) thanks to 3,010 career hits and 1,412 walks. But I thought the whole purpose of WAR was supposedly to establish an all-around value to a player, and 26 places further down on the all-time list you'll find one Joseph Paul DiMaggio with a WAR of 79.1. In other words, the WARmongers maintain Boggs was a far better all-around player—with slightly more than 12 wins above replacement—than DiMaggio.

The analytics geeks hate the traditional stats, which are mostly missing in their compilations of WAR. One such stat, which Buck Showalter once told me was for him the most important stat of them all, is games played. That brings me to another new favorite phrase of analytics: *load management*, the term they use for resting players. It's been determined by the analytics army that the solution to helping players avoid injuries is to give them periodic days off. But it's really another erosion of the managers' control over the lineups.

When Showalter was first being interviewed for the New York Mets managing job in December 2021, he was asked by their analytics geeks about his thoughts on load management, to which he replied: "The Atlanta Braves." After initial queried looks on their faces, it was pointed out that the entire Braves 2021 infield of Freddie Freeman, Ozzie Albies, Dansby Swanson, and Austin Riley played 156 or more games. Then in September of 2023, load management reared its ugly head on Showalter after his center fielder Brandon Nimmo had one of the best games of his career with two doubles and a triple. The next day as Showalter was putting together his lineup, the analytics staffers came to him and said he needed to give Nimmo a day-game-after-a-night-game load management day off because of all the extra activity he'd had on the basepaths the night before. "I didn't quite understand that one," Showalter said. "I said: 'What do you want me to tell him: Don't get any hits so you can play the next day?' You go out and tell Brandon Nimmo he's not playing today because he did too well last night."

As long as I've gone this far with my front porch rant on analytics, I might as well take it all the way by destroying the myth of the two poster franchises for cutting-edge analytics success: the 2015–2024 Houston Astros and 2023 Baltimore Orioles. On a January morning in 2019, Mike Elias, the newly minted general manager of the Orioles, and his top assistant, sabermetric guru Sig Mejdal, assembled the team's scouts for an indoctrination of philosophy meeting in the home team clubhouse at Camden Yards. But before the session was even halfway over, the scouts had come to the realization the meeting was actually a means for Elias to explain to them why they would soon all be fired. With their own formulas and metrics right there in their own database, they had everything they needed regarding the June draft.

Mejdal told them: "The players we've flagged in our data system are the ones we like, and if they're not flagged, you don't need to bother with them." In addition, he said when it came to pitchers, especially, the scouts no longer needed to watch them. "We have our own formula with pitchers."

Elias and Mejdal would not disclose how or from where all this data had been gathered, though it was assumed by the scouts it could not have been from actual firsthand observations of the players or the just-as-important, after-hours makeup evaluations that are a part of scouting, including interviews with the player's family, coaches, school officials, and counselors. Said Doug Witt, one of a dozen or so people at the meeting: "What they were essentially saying was 'we don't need you,' and we knew no matter what we said we'd be told we were wrong. So nobody spoke up. Whatever their formula for pitchers was, they kept it a secret."

Seven months later Elias announced the firing of 11 members of the team's scouting and front-office departments, including Jimmy Howard, a scout for 30 years in the Orioles organization and a member of the Professional Scouts Hall of Fame, and Dean Albany and Tripp Norton, who'd both held various scouting and player development positions in 20 years with the team. Meanwhile, one of Elias' first orders of business after taking over as Orioles baseball operations chief was the hiring of Tom Eller in January 2019 as the

Orioles' director of hitting. Eller, who never played professional baseball, had previously been the head baseball coach at Hartford (Maryland) Community College, where his team finished first in the nation in home runs (137 in 62 games) in 2017 and third in 2016. However, not so prominently listed on his resume was this other fact: in his 13 years at Hartford, Eller's hitters consistently led the nation in strikeouts.

According to a person who was present during part of Eller's interview with Elias in December 2018, the session—and Eller's demeanor in particular—bordered on the bizarre. Elias and Mejdal were intrigued by all the home runs Eller's teams generated, and the upper-cut swing approach he espoused as the crux of his philosophy. Squirming back and forth in his seat, Eller told the two Orioles execs: "I found the program online. Basically, it's swinging up and letting it fly. It worked for us."

At that point, Elias and Mejdal dismissed the Orioles hitting coaches from the meeting, and the next time any of them saw Eller was in spring training. According to one of the Orioles coaches, Eller was late for the batting practice drills half the time and didn't interact at all with Orioles hitting instructors Jeff Manto, Milt May, Butch Davis, and Keith Bodie, who had combined for more than 100 years of professional experience working with hitters.

At the first meeting with all the hitters, Eller sat in the back of the room, texted on his cell phone, and paid no attention to what was being said. He clearly had his own agenda, and it didn't include them—as Manto discovered much to his astonishment and dismay when he came out early one day and saw Eller had set up an L-screen 15 feet from the plate for the purpose of the hitters getting faster into their upper-cut swings in order to lift balls over it. Enraged, Manto raced over, threw the screen to the ground, and screamed: "I don't want to see that thing again!"

Right there, his days were numbered in the organization. Later, the coaches watched in bemusement as Eller, attempting to throw batting practice, had trouble getting his pitches to the plate and finally walked away, turning it over to the pitching machine, which the batters hated.

Elias and Mejdal were the disciples of Jeff Luhnow, who is generally regarded in baseball circles as the grand patriarch of analytics, first introducing them in a full-scale manner as the assistant general manager and player development director with the St. Louis Cardinals from 2003 to 2011 and then winning universal acclaim for rebuilding the Astros into world champions in 2017—a title that was later severely compromised by a sign-stealing cheating scandal.

Bodie, who worked as a minor league manager and instructor for both the Astros and the Orioles, provided further insight into the analytical kingdom over which Luhnow, Elias, and Mejdal presided. Luhnow was eight months into his first year as Astros general manager when on August 19, 2012 he fired his manager, Brad Mills. That was no surprise as the 55-year-old Mills had been essentially serving as a caretaker for a team undergoing a major rebuilding job and one that was headed for a second straight 100-loss season after Luhnow had traded off most of their higher-salaried veterans.

What was somewhat surprising was Luhnow's choice a month later of Bo Porter, the third-base coach for the Washington Nationals, as the new Astros manager. Though well regarded as an instructor and coach with the Nationals, Porter had very limited actual managerial experience—two years in the low minors—but as Bodie so noted, that was not a necessity. "They called him in and spelled it out to him what they wanted. They said: 'If we send down the lineup card every day, are you gonna be okay with that?' Bo said that would not be a problem and he got the job."

The other term of employment Porter accepted was knowing the Astros were deliberately tanking so as to benefit from getting high picks in the amateur draft. No matter how badly the Astros played, he understood Luhnow would be doing nothing to improve the team until the time was right. But after slogging through a 111-loss first season in 2012 and being at the continual mercy of Luhnow's analytics department, Porter became increasingly frustrated his second year and finally decided to go over Luhnow's head to Astros owner Jim Crane, whom he hoped would be sympathetic to his contention that he simply couldn't manage this way. Instead, Crane called Luhnow and informed him that his manager had essentially just thrown him under the bus, and a few days later, Porter was fired.

Luhnow replaced Porter with A.J. Hinch, who'd been a failure (89–123) in two years as manager of the Arizona Diamondbacks in 2009–10. Delighted at getting a second chance, Hinch also dutifully went along with the program. Three years later, as the beneficiary of those first-round draft choices—center fielder George Springer, shortstop Carlos Correa, and third baseman Alex Bregman—that were the result of finishing last three years in a row he led the Astros to the 2017 world championship.

Though the Astros under Luhnow's analytics revolution may have been hailed as the new state-of-the-art franchise in baseball, there is absolutely nothing to suggest this new-age data-driven player evaluation strategy had anything to do with the composition of their 2017 and 2019 championship teams. Yes, the decision to tear down the team and tank for four years enabled the Luhnow/Elias/Mejdal team to make no-brainer No. 1 draft picks on future franchise players Correa, Bregman, and Lance McCullers. But when they had the overall No. 1

draft picks in 2012, 2013, and 2014, they erred badly on both Stanford right-handed starter Mark Appel in 2013 and left-handed San Diego high school pitcher Brady Aiken in 2014. Aiken never made the majors, and Appel only appeared in six games—with the Philadelphia Phillies in 2022—before retiring. And in 2012 the Astros nearly blew it with Correa, the 17-year-old shortstop wunderkind from Puerto Rico whom Luhnow was prepared to pass over for Appel, then a college junior. According to the Astros scouts at the time, Luhnow was obsessed with Appel. "I don't know exactly what it was: his body type, that he threw a mid-90s fastball, or the fact that he was a Stanford kid with presumably superior smarts," one scout said.

What ultimately became the deciding factor was money. The overall No. 1 pick in 2012 carried a bonus slot value of $7.2 million. Luhnow first felt out Appel's advisor, Scott Boras, to ascertain the possibility of a discount. Boras refused, Appel fell to the Pittsburgh Pirates at No. 8, refused to sign with them, and then went back to Stanford. At the same time, Luhnow learned that Correa was willing to sign for $4.8 million, and with the savings of nearly $2.5 million, the Astros were then able to sign McCullers, the standout right-handed pitcher from Jesuit High in Tampa, Florida, who had fallen from a likely top 10 draftee all the way to 41 because he had made a verbal commitment to the University of Florida.

The No. 41 pick carried a slot value of only $1.26 million, and Luhnow got him to sign for $2.5 million. So for a total of $8.3 million, he got two first-round draft picks for a little more than a million dollars over the slot figure for the overall No. 1. Luhnow was hailed for pulling off one of the greatest draft coups in history—but not for any analytics-driven evaluation expertise—only because Boras refused to give him a discount on Appel.

As for the other key players on those Houston teams, Springer was a first-round draft pick—but by Luhnow's predecessor, Ed Wade. Jose Altuve, the American League Most Valuable Player in 2017, was signed as an international free agent also by Wade in 2007 (and at 5'6" almost certainly would have been rejected by Mejdal's database) while frontline starting pitchers Verlander, Charlie Morton, Zack Greinke, and Gerrit Cole and closers Ken Giles and Roberto Osuna were all established pitchers acquired in trades. In particular, certified aces Verlander and Greinke were able to be acquired by Luhnow for next to nothing (a bunch of low-level minor leaguers who never made it) only because of his willingness to take on the enormous amounts of money left on their contracts.

So, in fact, it was the failure of his analytics wizards in scouting and player development to produce any of their own starting pitchers that forced Luhnow to have to trade with other clubs for the most important ingredient for a championship club. Whatever Mejdal's secret formula for pitchers, it missed the boat on successive No. 1 draft picks, Appel in 2013 and Aiken in 2014.

There's an age-old saying in baseball: "You can't scout desire," which Hall of Fame general manager Pat Gillick, architect of world championship teams in Toronto and Philadelphia, re-affirmed to me about Appel. Gillick was living in Seattle when Appel was pitching for Stanford and got to see him a few times while scouting the Pac-10 conference. Like a lot of other team execs, Gillick wondered about Appel's desire when on Boras' advice he spurned the Pirates' $3.8 million bonus offer in 2012 to return to Stanford for his senior year. At 6'5", 215 pounds, his pro-ready body type was certainly imposing, and his fastball consistently clocked in the mid-90s along with a hard slider. But as Gillick observed, he had difficulties pitching out of trouble. "I just didn't like his body language. I would never have drafted him," he said. "For all their numbers—fastball velocity and spin rates, strikeouts-to-walks ratio—there's no way to quantify fear."

Nevertheless, with the No. 1 overall pick again in 2013, Luhnow went back to Appel and this time signed him to a $6.35 million bonus, which was $1.5 million below the $7.8 million slot value but still substantially higher than the $3.8 million Appel turned down from the Pirates the year before when he had the leverage of returning to Stanford for his senior year. After compiling mediocre stats at Double A Corpus Christi and Triple A Fresno in 2015, Appel was traded by Luhnow to the Phillies. He continued to struggle at Triple A Lehigh Valley in 2016 and suffered a shoulder injury in 2017 before the Phillies released him.

Such was the same fate for Aiken, Luhnow's overall No. 1 pick in 2014. Acknowledging that they couldn't blow it a second year in a row with the top pick in the draft, Luhnow, Elias, Mejdal, and co. allowed *Sports Illustrated*'s Ben Reiter rare access to their draft room as they debated the merits (or rather the metrics) of the four finalists they were considering: left-hander Carlos Rodon of North Carolina State, who was regarded as the top college pitcher in the draft; high school right-hander Tyler Kolek from Shepherd, Texas; the left-hander Aiken from Cathedral Catholic High in San Diego; and Alex Jackson, a high school catcher from Southern California. After two days of intense debate, they finally settled on Aiken. "We decided the morning of the draft. The mere fact that we were willing to take a high school pitcher one-one for the third time in history, even though the first two didn't pan out, showed us how strongly we agreed," Reiter quoted Elias. "We didn't want to look back in 10 years and say: 'We passed on the best high school lefty ever just to get something a little quicker.'"

Unfortunately, Aiken turned out to be damaged goods, a fact that was not realized by the Astros until after they'd agreed to terms with him on a $6.5 million bonus, $1.5 million below the slot value for the No. 1 overall pick. During his routine post-draft physical, an MRI reportedly revealed a smaller-than-normal ulnar collateral ligament in his elbow. This prompted the Astros to reduce their bonus offer to $3.1 million. It was an offer Aiken and his agent, Casey Close, readily refused. By failing to sign Aiken, the Astros, much to the objections of the rest of the major league teams, were awarded with the second pick in the 2015 draft, which they used on Bregman. So they lucked out again.

When Elias and Mejdal moved on to Baltimore in 2018, they embarked on the same tanking formula as they'd used in Houston, and for the next four years, the Orioles became the embarrassment of baseball, losing 115 games in 2018, 108 games in '19, and 110 games in '21. After the 2021 season, Elias announced a rash of firings, including hitting coach Don Long and Gary Kendall, a highly respected minor league manager, coach, and instructor, who'd been with the organization for 21 years. The firing of Long was especially curious if only because the Orioles' hitting—in particular rookie first baseman Ryan Montcastle (33 home runs, 89 RBIs), Silver Slugger center fielder Cedric Mullins (.291 batting average, 30 home runs), left fielder Austin Hays (22 home runs, 71 RBIs), and designated hitter Trey Mancini (21 home runs, 71 RBIs)—was one of the few positives in their otherwise dreadful season. As Manto pointed out: "All four of those players were signed by the previous administration and honed their hitting skills with all the minor league coaches Elias fired."

In his 2021 postseason purge, Elias neglected to make public one other firing—that of Tom Eller, the hitting guru from Hartford Community College whose textbook, upper-cut hitting approach apparently was deemed not so cutting edge as it had been cracked up to be.

When the Orioles finally broke through with a 101-win first place season in the American League East in 2023, Elias was hailed by his peers as Major League Baseball Executive of the Year. But what exactly did he do? Catcher Adley Rutschman was a no-brainer, first-round draft pick in 2019 courtesy of tanking. Most of the rest of the core everyday players, Mountcastle, Mullins, Santander, and Hays were all signed by Elias' predecessor, Dan Duquette as were promising right-handed starter Grayson Rodriguez and closer Felix Bautista. Elias did make two nice pickups in first baseman Ryan O'Hearn and set-up man Yennier Cano, but when it came to acquiring a desperately needed frontline starting pitcher at the trading deadline, he came up empty, and that cost the Orioles dearly when they were swept 3–0 by the Texas Rangers in the first round of the playoffs.

So at the risk of being accused of baseball blasphemy, I would submit that the rise from the ashes by both the Luhnow-led Astros and Elias-directed Orioles had absolutely nothing to do with analytics and everything to do with subjecting their fans to five depressing years of tanking. When analytics was first taking hold in baseball in the early 2000s, its proponents maintained it was going to save the owners millions as all this advanced technology would enable them to make better decisions on players.

That sure hasn't happened. What analytics has done is add layers and layers of people up and down the organizations. For decades baseball had a limit of six coaches per team. Now there is seemingly no limit. In 2022 the San Francisco Giants had 16 coaches, only three of whom ever played major league ball. They finished at 81–81. In 2024 Elias had 14 people listed in the Orioles analytics department, including two with titles of junior data scientist. The New York Yankees had at least 20 analytics people at the major league level and a dozen more in their player development system. They also had 14 people listed in their health and performance staff, coming off a season in which Yankees players had the third most days lost to injury in the majors, 2,154, at a cost to the club of $82 million.

If I sound like an ornery Oscar the Grouch when it comes to analytics in baseball, it's because I am. I fail to see any way analytics has made baseball better other than providing extra layers of people with convoluted formulas and metrics to supposedly better evaluate players. I'm sorry, but I miss Whitey Ford versus Billy Pierce, Warren Spahn versus Robin Roberts, Koufax versus Juan Marichal, Jack Morris versus John Smoltz, Randy Johnson versus Pedro Martinez. And I miss the old-school managers with personality like Earl Weaver, Sparky Anderson, Bobby Cox, Joe Torre, Jim Leyland, Lou Piniella, and Terry Francona, who understood players were not statistical robots but had pulses—and loved nothing better than sitting in their offices prior to the games talking baseball with the writers instead of debating the analytics geeks about the lineup. Most of all I hate what analytics has done to the dedicated scouts, the heart and soul of baseball in my opinion, who are little by little being cast aside for the hordes of Ivy League mathematic geeks who never played the game at the professional level.

At the same time, I understand analytics is now the way of life in baseball, just like artificial intelligence is the way of life in the world, and there's no turning back from it. Because it's been ingrained in me from the time I was seven years old, baseball for me will always be the greatest game of them all. Or as Bob Lemon once said to me: "In spite of the people who run it." It's lost some of its wonderful simplicity and its personalities, and I worry about today's generation of fans not having the same appreciation for its lore and its history as I did.

But the beauty of the game has always been its resilience, and having covered baseball from the advent of free agency—which the owners insisted would be its ruination—through numerous work stoppages, the cancellation of a World Series, and the scourge of steroids that made a mockery of its home run records, I remain confident it will also somehow manage to survive the invasion of analytics.

On to the next 150 years.

ACKNOWLEDGMENTS

W hen you've been blessed to enjoy the fruits of the exciting and rewarding profession for more than half a century as I have, you've had to have also been extremely fortunate to encounter and cultivate a lot of good people along the way who made you better at what you do. In that respect please indulge me because my list is lengthy.

It starts with my colleagues at the *New York Daily News*:

Buddy Martin and Dick Young, who hired me and then served as valuable mentors.

Teri Thompson, my boss (managing editor/sports from 2010 to 2015) and cohort on so many award-winning investigative pieces who became a dear friend and also helped edit many of my books.

Martin Dunn, two-time editor in chief at the *Daily News* who believed in my abilities to the point that I still owe him a 10 percent commission for wrangling the biggest raise I ever got at the paper out of publisher Mort Zuckerman. I was fortunate that our working relationship continued after Martin left the paper the second time to form his own production company, Street Smart Video, with his former *Daily*

News associate Marie McGovern, and we spent nearly three years collaborating on the 2019 documentary *Seaver*.

Leon Carter brought a welcome calm and sanity to the *Daily News* sports department as sports editor from 1999 to 2010 after years of difficult (to put it kindly) sports editors before him. We were a good team, and I appreciated that he respected my judgement when it came to hiring baseball beat writers.

The *Daily News* baseball beat writers, whom I affectionately called "My Team"—Anthony McCarron, Mark Feinsand, Kristie Ackert, Adam Rubin, Sam Borden, Roger Rubin, Christian Red, and especially Peter Botte, who skillfully got my candidacy for the Baseball Writers Association's J.G. Taylor Spink Award across the finish line and through the petty politics of the New York chapter in 2010.

My trusty compadre Bob Raisman, with whom I spent hundreds of Fridays sharing laughs and bouncing off column ideas at the *Daily News* before adjourning to Elaine's for nights of unwinding and always unpredictable craziness. Those were some of the best times of my life. I love you, Pally.

Delores Thompson, confidant, best friend, and den mother to us all, who as assistant sports editor made sure our credentials were always waiting for us and who knew where all our "bodies were buried" and made sure they stayed there.

The tireless and unsung researchers in the *Daily News* library, whose assistance in all my books was invaluable. In particular, Vinny Panzarini, Faigi Rosenthal, Scott Widener, "Sheriff" Browne, Ellen Locker, Shirley Wong, Pete Edelman, Jo Barefoot, and Jimmy Converso.

And away from the *Daily News*:

Hall of Fame basketball coach Frank McGuire, the Godfather of my career.

Roland Hemond, the sweetest, smartest, and most generous person I've ever known in baseball. There's a reason he was the second person (after Buck himself) to win the Hall of Fame's Buck O'Neil Lifetime Achievement Award. He epitomized what the award is all about: "an individual whose extraordinary efforts enhanced baseball's positive impact on society, broadened the game's appeal and whose character, integrity, and dignity are comparable to the namesake of the award." In his nearly 25 years as general manager of the Chicago White Sox and the Baltimore Orioles, Roland made 183 trades involving a total of 654 players and had a story (often quite humorous) for all of them, which he shared amid much frivolity at our annual Sunday night dinners at the Hall of Fame. I learned so much from Roland and had so much fun with him. I cherish his memory.

Jack Griffin, who gave me my first job in the business at United Press International without having read a single thing I'd ever written.

Milton Richman, Fred Down, Bob Stewart, and Fred McMane, my first mentors at United Press International, who taught me the ropes of writing on deadline and the art of creative leads.

Moss Klein, my treasured friend and co-author of *Damned Yankees* and whose company we kept for 18 years on the New York Yankees beat and who later became a proofreader extraordinaire on all my baseball books. There is no one in my profession I respected more.

Bill Francis, my go-to guy at the Hall of Fame whose research assistance for all of my books was invaluable.

Jeff Idelson, Art Berke, Rick Cerrone, and Marty Appel, valued friends all who on occasion also became valuable sources for which I am not at liberty to disclose.

Yankees President Randy Levine, whose encouragement and "releasing of the hostages" was essential to my being able to write *Steinbrenner: The Last Lion of Baseball*.

Elaine Kaufman, whose wise counsel and unconditional generosity meant everything to me.

Fellow New York scribes Dom Amore, Pete Caldera, and Ira Berkow who never failed to support me.

The guys at the Elias Sports Bureau and later other statistical services—Steve and Tom Hirdt, John Labombarda, and Bob Waterman, who never failed to help.

Acknowledgments

My extreme thanks to Tom Reichert, the dean of journalism at the University of South Carolina, who 50 years later facilitated my being able to attain those last four credits for my degree that I'd left behind in 1970 when I got my first job at UPI in New York.

Jeff Fedotin, my editor at Triumph, who "got" this book and guided it seamlessly to fruition.

Rob Wilson, my longtime agent and friend with whom I've had a wonderful working relationship for 25 years and six books.

And lastly, any measure of success I may have had in the writing profession could not have been achieved without the strong support of family, and in that respect, I have been truly blessed with my son, Steven Madden; my stepson, Christopher Longinetti; my sister, Jennie, who always promoted me; and my wife and life partner, Lillian.

INDEX